"We have never before had a President who admitted authorizing burglary. We have never had a President who admitted he obstructed justice. We have never had a President who tried to steal a national election," concludes Nixon scholar Leonard Lurie. Beyond all reasonable doubt Richard Nixon merits impeachment.

The Nixon Administration set out deliberately, knowingly, in a systematic way to subvert and destroy the very processes through which American democracy must operate. The most important act of this democracy is the quadrennial choice of a President. As historian Arthur Link states, "It is the most important act of sovereignty that people can exercise." To subvert this act is a high crime.

# The
# Impeachment
## of
## Richard
# Nixon

## LEONARD LURIE

A BERKLEY MEDALLION BOOK
published by
BERKLEY PUBLISHING CORPORATION

SBN 425-02443-1

BERKLEY MEDALLION BOOKS are published by
Berkley Publishing Corporation
200 Madison Avenue
New York, N. Y. 10016

BERKLEY MEDALLION BOOKS ® TM 757,375

Printed in the United States of America

Berkley Medallion Edition, June, 1973

# Contents

# CHAPTER I

## *The History of Impeachment, with One Omission*

For over two decades the public has followed the twists and turns of Richard Nixon's always obsessively ambitious career, a career occasionally marked by criminal activity, often stained by sleaziness bordering on corruption. During this time his foes have hoped and expected that American idealism—and the process of democratic elections—would deal him the fate he has always so richly deserved.

In the spring of 1972, the former investigative reporter Randolph Phillips spearheaded an advertising campaign to arouse interest in impeaching the President. It was obvious Phillips' motivation rested on political antagonism against Nixon's Vietnam policy. However, a political difference of opinion is no basis for impeachment.

In 1868 Senator Lyman Trumbull, an Illinois Republican, expressed this point of view when he explained the reason he had broken party discipline and voted against Andrew Johnson's impeachment:

"Once set the example of impeaching a President for what, when the excitement of the hour shall have subsided, will be regarded as insufficient cause, and no future President will be safe who happens to differ with a majority of the House and two thirds of the Senate on any measure deemed by them important, particularly if of a political character."

In 1972 the grounds for impeachment seemed completely lacking. A distaste for Nixon's style, a gut conviction that he was untrustworthy, and a passionate opposition to his conduct of the Vietnam war were disagreements largely political. We were also quite close to the election and, it was felt "the American jury" was shortly going to be given the opportunity to vote on the Nixon question.

When that vote was in all but the most rabid Nixon haters placed the matter behind them, never entertaining the thought that anyone but Richard Nixon would be our President for the next four years. The major regret was that the kingmakers of the Democratic and Republican parties had presented the American people with what was, for the vast majority of them, two such unpalatable choices.

Easter Week of 1973 tipped much of the nation's thinking in the opposite direction. For ten months the Watergate scandal had dominated the front pages. Despite the constant efforts of Nixon and his associates to play down the importance of the Democratic headquarters break-in—and, indeed, to picture the brouhaha arising from each new revelation as a conspiracy by the liberal press to undermine confidence in the Republican party and weaken the Presidency—it was clear that increasing numbers of Americans were convinced serious criminal behavior had taken place.

When on Tuesday, April 17, Nixon read a statement to the press indicating that he now believed "there have been major developments in the case" which might lead to persons in the executive branch being "indicted," it became apparent that we were being confronted with something unique in American history. When he went on to say, "I condemn any attempts to cover up in this case, no matter who is involved," he was defining the obvious, and only, standard which should guide anyone concerned with the truth and the future of American political institutions.

Thoughts of impeachment rose naturally from Nixon's revelation. It was time then to turn to Article II, Section 4 of the Constitution, which deals with the House of Representatives' power to impeach (indict) and the Senate's power to try suspected governmental officials so impeached by the House.

It is short and extremely explicit. "The President, Vice-President, and all civil officers of the United States, shall be removed from office on impeachment for, and conviction of, treason, bribery, or other high crimes and misdemeanors."

The men who wrote the Constitution concerned themselves with broad matters of structure. It is a relatively short document. The inclusion of a Presidential impeachment clause cannot, therefore, have been a casual decision. They envisioned a day when *some* President would be guilty of "treason, bribery, or other high crimes and misdemeanors," and they meant to provide for a way to remove that individual from office.

However, a Senator, Tennessee's William Blount, has the distinction of suffering the first impeachment. Blount served in the Revolutionary War and was a signer of the Constitution. He was territorial governor in 1790 and, when Tennessee became a state in 1796, he became its first Senator.

Blount was a man of strong convictions. On July 7, 1797 he was impeached by a majority vote in the House of Representatives. The charge was he had conspired to wage war with Spain in favor of Great Britain. He was also accused of attempting to stir up the Cherokee Indians against Spain and the United States. He was expelled from the Senate almost immediately, since the members of that body have the power to determine the qualification of their colleagues. However, the process of impeachment, representing *terra incognita,* continued as though he were still a member of that body.

His trial in the Senate lasted from December 17, 1798, to January 14, 1799. Blount based his defense on the legalism that he was not a "civil" officer of the United States. The treasonous aspects of his conduct were somewhat blunted by the fact that we had become involved in an undeclared naval war with Great Britain's chief enemy, France. As a gesture to logic, since Blount was no longer in the Senate, the charges against him were dismissed by his former colleagues "for lack of jurisdiction."

Despite the clouded procedural aspects of this first impeachment trial, there is no doubt it was pursued within the meaning of the Constitution. Treason is a specific ground for impeachment, and treason was the substance of the charge against Blount.

The second impeachment charge was for good cause, but resulted in a good deal of squirming by the Senators who sat in judgment. The proceedings against Federal District Judge John Pickering were started by Thomas Jefferson. On February 3, 1803, the President sent a message to Congress, accompanied by documents, drawing the attention of that body to the conduct of this New Hampshire judge. The House promptly acted on Jefferson's call for "proceedings of redress."

Jefferson's documents focused on one particular case handled by Pickering, although the judge had exhibited similar conduct for the previous three years. He was accused of malfeasance and unlawful conduct, and was described as a man of loose morals and intemperate habits, who frequently donned his robes while "in a state of total intoxication." Furthermore, he had "frequently, in a most profane and indecent manner, invoke[d] the name of the Supreme Being."

It appears the judge was insane. At least that was the opinion of those who knew him best, including his son, who filed a deposition identifying his father as a lunatic.

There were two matters which distressed those seeking a conviction. The charges against Pickering were not clearly delineated in the impeachment clause. Since he was not guilty of "treason, bribery or high crimes," Jefferson's friends were forced to fall back on the allegation that he was, at least, guilty of a misdemeanor.

Also disturbing some tender consciences was the fact that Pickering was being pursued, at least in part, because he was a Federalist. Jefferson and his Democratic-Republicans had won the election of 1800 only to discover that John Adams had loaded the federal bench with Federalist stalwarts, appointed for a lifetime. At this early stage in our national development some of Jefferson's supporters insisted that impeachment was the proper method of ridding the judiciary of the opposition party, which had been defeated in the previous election. Jefferson's men were philosophic democrats and did not smile upon a theory that gave lifetime jobs, and something approaching monarchal status, to members of a party with whom the voters no longer agreed.

Senator Dayton described the dilemma of his colleagues: "There were members who were disposed to give sentence of removal . . . who could not, however, conscientiously vote that they [the proved facts] amounted to high crimes and misdemeanors, especially when committed by a man proved at the very time to be insane, and to have been so ever since . . ."

In order to avoid voting "aye or no" on the facts in each article of the charge, nineteen *yeas* overcame seven *nays* to find befuddled Pickering "guilty as charged."

The Constitutional scholar Andrew C. McLaughlin maintains that, by doing this, the Senate avoided "an explicit announcement of its right to remove an officer for acts not technically criminal."

With this first successful impeachment, which did not find its justification in precise language in the Constitution, the scope of future proceedings was immensely broadened. In effect, a governmental officer was susceptible to impeachment if Congress charged him with conduct unworthy of his office. The Pickering impeachment established that there were few limits on the authority of Congress to remove individuals against whom fifty per cent of the House and two-thirds of the Senate wished to act.

The third impeachment attempted to nail down this concept. Supreme Court Justice Samuel Chase, a man of no mean talents and many mean opinions, was impeached in 1803. Justice Chase partook in none of the evil practices which led Pickering to his destruction, save the immoderate expression of his Federalist point of view. He was in the habit of flailing out at Jefferson in the midst of an ordinary court day. This inappropriate behavior might have been overlooked at another time, but the Federalists and Anti-Federalists were at each other's throats precisely at the moment Chase decided to make a most inflammatory statement.

Universal suffrage, he opined, while charging a Baltimore grand jury, will "rapidly destroy all protection to property, and all security to personal liberty; and our republican constitution will sink into a mobocracy, the worst of all possible governments."

Keep in mind that by "universal suffrage" Chase did not mean to include slaves and women; it never occurred to him that either group deserved the vote he enjoyed. Determined to make his position perfectly clear, he imperiously declared to the stunned jurors that "the modern doctrines by our late reformers, that all men in a state of society are entitled to enjoy equal liberty and equal rights, have brought this mighty mischief upon us. . . ."

The cry went up from Congress—now in complete control of the Anti-Federalists—to do to Chase what they had just finished doing to Pickering. No doubt Chase had behaved injudiciously. However, was that reason enough to remove him from office? Did anyone believe his outburst was even a misdemeanor, in the sense that was meant by the Founding Fathers?

As an indication of how far the doctrine of impeachment had come in such a short time, it is only necessary to examine some of the language of the eight articles brought against him. He was accused of conducting one trial "in a manner highly arbitrary, oppressive, and unjust." In another case the indictment accused him of "unbecoming conduct and disregard of law," a charge frequently made by lawyers who have been on the wrong end of a judicial ruling.

The trial began on January 2, 1805. The managers of the Senate were determined to make a grand showing of their power. They decked the benches of the Senate in scarlet cloth and prepared to deal with Chase as they had with Pickering.

The central question, one that has special meaning in the context of the Watergate crimes, was what constituted an impeachable offense. Chase's counsel, the brilliant and loquacious Luther Martin, nicknamed "the Federalist bulldog," insisted that, in order to convict, the offense had to be indictable. The Senators might not like what Chase had said, and they might even consider him reprehensible; but conviction depended on finding him "in violation of *some law*." If the Senate was to find Chase guilty of a misdemeanor, they must not merely determine he was guilty of *misbehavior,* a term synonymous in the dictionary with misdemeanor; rather, they must conclude such misbehavior was "a violation of some law punishable."

Thirty-four members were present on March 1, 1805. Twenty-three votes were required for conviction. The eighth and last article, concerned with his stellar performance in Baltimore, received the highest count, nineteen. Chase was returned to his courtroom podium from which he delivered many more opinions, both legal and personal.

His impeachment seems to have lent support to the theory that conviction of an official should not be for partisan purposes. However, that theory—if indeed it was the major conclusion to be drawn from this event—won out by only four votes. It would have been unwise for some intemperate Solon without Chase's undeniable ability and reputation for honesty to depend on a repetition of Senatorial generosity.

However, the disposition to resort to impeachment was cooled, and it was not until 1830 that another attempt was made. At that time a Missouri lawyer with the improbable name Luke Lawless had written a newspaper article excoriating a decision by District Judge James Peck. Peck was not one to endure insult in silence. He had Lawless hauled into his presence and instantly decided he was in contempt of court—which apparently reflected Lawless's own feelings about the judge. Recognizing the evil nature of the miscreant standing unrepentant before his bar, Peck sentenced Lawless to jail for twenty-four hours and ordered him to stay away from his law books for eighteen months.

Although Peck was acquitted by the Senate, January,

1831, Congress was so concerned about what it considered to be an attack on the freedom of the press that it passed a law specifying contempt of court only for offenses that happened in the presence of the judge, or in such proximity to the courthouse that they resulted in the obstruction of justice.

Not until 1862, in the midst of the Civil War, was a judge to be tried for a charge resembling treason. West H. Humphreys, a District Court Judge in Tennessee, was impeached for supporting the secessionists. He was convicted and removed from office.

There have since been eight attempts at impeachment. Six involved judges. The last ensnared Halsted L. Ritter of Florida, who was removed from office on April 17, 1936. The frequency of judicial impeachment can be explained by the fact that judges serve for life. Civil officers can be removed by political office holders who are themselves dependent on the periodic approval of a fickle electorate.

By 1913 the grounds for impeachment of judges had been expanded to the point where ex-President William Howard Taft was able to tell the American Bar Association that, "By the liberal interpretation of the term 'high misdemeanor,' which the Senate has given it, there is now no difficulty in securing the removal of a judge for any reason that shows him unfit. . . ."

Of the two remaining impeachment trials, one concerned a Cabinet officer, William W. Belknap, Secretary of War during Grant's sordid administration. In 1876 he was impeached on the Constitutional charge of accepting bribes, a not uncommon crime during that era of Boss Tweed and Jay Gould. Being a prudent man who prided himself on knowing the value of things, Belknap rushed to his friend Grant, waving his resignation and crying out, "They can't impeach you if you resign first, can they?" The charges against him were dropped.

Although there have been hundreds of thousands of federal office holders in the history of our nation, only thirteen times has the House of Representatives brought itself to the extremity of impeachment. In all that time only four impeachments have succeeded. Only once have charges been aimed at a President. It is that case to which members of Congress and American citizens must now look for guidance.

# CHAPTER II

## *The Omission*

Andrew Johnson, the seventeenth President of the United States, was a man of exceptional bravery and self-confidence, whose life seemed to validate his countrymen's faith in democracy. He grew up as a "poor white" Southerner. Born in some other land, Johnson would have been too perceptive for the needs of his ordinary life, probably short-tempered with his more unimaginative fellows, and constantly suspect in the eyes of the local squire. But raised in egalitarian Tennessee, where Jacksonian Democracy was an article of faith, Johnson was able to take advantage of the mobile social structure to advance on his merits.

He was trained as an apprentice tailor, and practiced that trade for many years. It was not until after he was married that his wife taught him how to read and write. Johnson, nevertheless, was a born intellectual with a flair for stump speaking. He served for thirty years as Governor of Tennessee, Congressman and Senator. It was the Civil War that tested his courage and revealed the most durable qualities of the man.

In 1861, as his fellow Southerners stood up in the Senate to denounce Lincoln and departed into the ranks of the secessionists, Johnson remained at his desk, convinced that the Constitution had set up a government worthy of defense. The following year Lincoln appointed him military governor of Tennessee, where he was the target of assassin's bullets and was forced to defend a territory surrounded by Confederate troops.

Lincoln chose him as Vice-Presidential nominee for his reelection campaign in 1864. Although they were similar in many respects, notably in background, they were sharply different in temperament. Lincoln was a

18

compromiser. He had even been willing to allow slavery in the South after his first election in order to avoid Civil War. He cajoled recalcitrants and disguised the seriousness of his purpose with jokes.

Johnson was more direct. The possessor of a temper, he was capable of venting his emotions without ceremony.

Lincoln's assassination on April 14, 1865, was a shock to all—but to the Radical Republican majority in Congress, it had its redeeming aspects. Lincoln had proposed leniency toward the defeated South. As far as he was concerned, if the rebelling states accepted the Thirteenth Amendment outlawing slavery and agreed to swear loyalty to the United States and its laws, they could reenter the Union.

The Radical Republicans detested the thought that this might happen. A war had been fought, and hundreds of thousands of Northerners had died; surely the rebels had to pay a price—and not merely a token price.

Johnson's first statements after the assassination was a call for revenge. The culprits must be captured and executed. Ohio's Senator Benjamin F. Wade, soon to be one of Johnson's chief tormentors, cried out, "There will be no trouble now running this government."

The elation of the Radicals, who had opposed Lincoln with increasing vigor during the previous year, was quickly dissipated. At his first Cabinet meeting Johnson declared his intentions to follow Lincoln's mild program of reconstruction. His decision to be magnanimous was secretly conveyed to the Congressional Radicals by Edwin M. Stanton, the Secretary of War, around whom the zealots for impeachment rallied.

Stanton was a bearded Pennsylvania lawyer who had served in Buchanan's and Lincoln's Cabinets. In public, it was his style to fawn on them. In private, he ridiculed them mercilessly. Stanton was a blackguard, in the fullest meaning of that favorite Victorian word. While assuring Johnson of his agreement with his reconstruction plans, he was constantly scheming with the Congressional Radicals to undermine them.

The chiefs of the Radicals were Senator Charles Sumner, who had been brutally caned by an outraged young Southerner in 1856 and was still simmering in unrelenting martyrdom, and sickly Congressman Thaddeus Stevens, who was seventy-three when Johnson took office. Stevens was grimly determined to spend his last days on earth cauterizing the wounds of rebellion. A man with a severely deformed foot and an easily provoked spleen, his dedication to the anti-slavery movement was unmatched in the Congress. As a symbol of his determination, he had purchased a plot in a Negro cemetery, in which his interment was shortly to take place.

Precipitating the quarrel between these strong-minded men was the President's veto of the Civil Rights Act of 1866.

Although the Thirteenth Amendment outlawed "slavery" and "involuntary servitude," it exempted involuntary servitude "as a punishment for crime whereof the party shall have been duly convicted . . ." Bitter-enders in the South seized upon this language to justify a back-door effort to reimpose slavery. They passed "black codes" by means of which rootless black men, a quality naturally shared by most black men at the time of emancipation, would be considered vagrants. So classified, they were arrested by local sheriffs and, *duly convicted,* were fined and placed in jail. Since these black "criminals" were penniless, they were unable to gain their release.

There was no shortage of white benefactors, all former slave holders, who were willing to pay the fines of the ex-slaves. All they required was a sheriff's paper committing the black prisoner to a specified period of "service," theoretically long enough only to repay the benefactor's generosity.

In an effort to end this practice, Sumner and Stevens had rushed through their Civil Rights Act. They were astounded when Johnson returned it with a veto message citing the Constitution and claiming the law was a "stride towards centralization and the concentration of all legislative powers in the national government."

Equally decent men frequently come down on different sides of an issue. In his veto message, Johnson argued that his objections had been taken on legal points but insisted that his continuing determination was to give meaning to emancipation. He said he would "cheerfully co-operate" with any civil rights legislation "compatible with the Constitution."

There is little doubt Johnson had let his antipathy for Radical Republican proposals obscure the genuine need for overcoming Southern opposition to black equality. However, deluded as he was, he rested easily in the White House, convinced he had permanently dispatched the issue.

Supporting this conviction was the fact that Congress had never overridden a veto of a major bill. However, Sumner proclaimed a new day when he announced that "by assassination of Abraham Lincoln the Rebellion was vaulted into the Presidential chair." Before the end of his term Congress had overturned fifteen out of eighteen Johnson vetos.

Efforts to impeach Johnson began seriously in 1867. The Radical Republicans controlled more than two-thirds in each house. In an effort to lay the groundwork for impeachment and, in effect, to entrap the President, the Radicals placed a rider on the Army Appropriations Act, requiring Johnson to send all his orders to field commanders through Ulysses S. Grant, then General of the Armies. Any violation of the rider was to be considered "a misdemeanor in office."

In order to draw the noose tighter around him, the Tenure of Office Act was passed over his veto. This act was simple in its aim. Any official who had been approved by the Senate was to serve until the Senate approved his successor. Furthermore, and more to the point, Cabinet officers were to "hold their offices respectively for and during the term of the President by whom they may have been appointed," unless removed by the Senate.

Since Johnson was beginning to understand the depths of Stanton's treachery, the wily Secretary of War was anxious to gain the protection of Congress. To make the ultimate meaning of the Radical Republicans clear, the following language appeared: "Every removal, appointment, or employment" contrary to its provisions "shall be deemed . . . a *high misdemeanor*." A constitutional trap was being set for the President.

A more cautious man might have pulled back at this point. However, Johnson viewed himself as being in the right, and much abused by ruthless enemies. In recommending a veto, the Cabinet—including an extremely vociferous Stanton—claimed the act was clearly unconstitutional and required a court challenge.

It is important to remember that Johnson had precedent on his side. Since the time of Washington, Cabinet officers served at the pleasure of the President. When they outlived their usefulness, he replaced them without any reference to the Senate.

Still posing as the President's friend, Stanton explained why that arrangement was necessary: "Any man who would retain his seat in the Cabinet when his advice was not wanted was unfit for the place."

It was from such hypocrisy that the impeachment of Andrew Johnson proceeded. A first attempt was made in the late fall of 1867. The House voted 108 to 39 to authorize an inquiry by the Judiciary Committee "into the official conduct of Andrew Johnson." After 1,200 pages of testimony the committee recommended impeachment. In the House debate which ensued, it became apparent that the Judiciary Committee had based its conclusions on the opinion that Johnson disliked Congress and liked Southern rebels. Still somewhat in control of their passions, the House voted down the resolution 108 to 57.

A few days later, Johnson—who had endured Stanton's more brazen defiances since the passage of the Tenure of Office Act—informed the Senate that he had discharged the Secretary of War. He filed this report in accordance with the provisions of the Tenure Act, dutifully stating reasons for Stanton's suspension.

The Senate was enflamed. Without any real sign of opposition it passed a resolution restoring Stanton to office. The gauntlet thrown by Johnson had been picked up and was being hurled back in his face.

In January, 1868, Stanton resumed his duties. Johnson held his fire for five weeks, but on February 21 he ordered General Lorenzo Thomas to take over the War Department. Thomas subsequently described what happened when he handed Stanton Johnson's order to vacate his office.

"He then said, 'I do not know whether I will obey your instructions or whether I will resist them.' . . . I said that I should issue orders as Secretary of War. He said that I should not; he would countermand them, and he turned to General Schriver and also to General Townsend, who were in the room, and directed them not to obey any orders coming from me as Secretary of War. . . . The first thing that happened to me next morning was the appearance at my house of the Marshal of the District, with an assistant marshal and a constable, and he arrested me. . . . He went with me to the President's and went into the room where the President was. I stated that I had been arrested. . . . He said, 'Very well, that is the place I want it in—the courts.' "

Johnson was convinced his view of the unconstitutionality of the Tenure of Office Act would be upheld, if only it could be brought to the attention of the judiciary. Stanton, Sumner and Stevens agreed with him, and therefore made every effort to escape such adjudication. To avoid the court test, Stanton's attorneys moved for discharge of their complaint against Thomas.

The matter was now where the Radical Republicans wanted it, in the hands of Congress. On February 24, within three days of Thomas' confrontation with Stanton, the House, under the whip of Thaddeus Stevens, passed the first resolution for Presidential impeachment. The debate had been riotous. Washington was in an uproar. Wild accusations that Johnson had been involved in Lincoln's assassination were voiced. The vote was overwhelming, 126–47, and any hope Johnson might have of better treatment from the Senate seemed unrealistic.

While Stanton bivouacked in his office, determined to hold out against any surprise attack from the President, the House drew up eleven articles of impeachment. The first eight charges were rambling; whatever focus they had concentrated on the charge that Johnson had violated the Tenure of Office Act. The trap had been sprung. Article Nine accused Johnson of having an unlawful "conversation" with General William H. Emory, Army Commander for the District of Columbia, in an attempt to induce him to accept an order from him without first channeling it through Grant's office, as Congress had directed in the rider to the Army Appropriation Act.

Article Ten was a bad joke concocted by turncoat Democrat Ben Butler. In 1860, at the Democrats' Presidential convention, Butler had voted thirty-seven times for the nomination of Jefferson Davis. Once having seen the light, Butler became unrelenting in his pursuit of anyone he suspected of Southern sympathies. His chief suspicions had come to settle on the President of the United States. In Butler's article was recorded many of the foolish things Johnson had said in the heat of battle. In the 1866 Congressional campaign Johnson had frequently cursed the Radicals, using some of the choicest language learned in his hard youth. The result was a loss of dignity. No one doubted Johnson could make a fool of himself, but was that an impeachable offense?

The one story most often told about him related an event which took place when he was inaugurated as Lincoln's Vice-President. Reaching for some cheap courage, he had fortified himself with two slugs of brandy prior to rising for his ceremonial speech. He spoke with such a level of incoherence that political leaders nearby grabbed at his coattails in an effort to make him sit down. This incident left him with an undeserved reputation for public drunkenness.

Butler's article was all-encompassing. In it he accused Johnson of "utterances, declarations, threats, and harangues" so vile as to be "peculiarly indecent . . . in the Chief Magistrate of the United States." Johnson, he sanctimoniously averred, had brought the Presidential office "into contempt, ridicule, and disgrace."

It was the eleventh article, the so-called "Omnibus Article," drawn up by Stevens with all the care and bile at his command, on which the hopes of Johnson's enemies rested. It accused Johnson of unconstitutional "declarations." Furthermore, he was charged with trying to prevent use of the Tenure of Office Act. It also accused him of violating the Reconstruction Act of March 2, 1867.

Just as Article Ten had been a gossip catch-all, Article Eleven was a legal catch-all. It was as though by repetition Stevens expected to have his way.

The weakness of the charges was immediately apparent. With the exception of Article Ten, they all rested on Johnson's alleged disregard for the Tenure of Office Act, an offense which only the most extreme partisans could think of as impeachable. The use of bad language, which seemed to offend cottonmouth Butler so much, likewise seemed a poor excuse for stripping the President of his office. As for Johnson's frequent denunciations of Congress, far from considering this grounds for impeachment, some men might have wanted to congratulate him for his good judgment. There was, in short, no language in the impeachment section of the Constitution which referred to poor judgment or bad taste.

Finally, although Johnson was accused of refusing to carry out the provisions of the Reconstruction Act, none of his accusers were able to point to a single instance of such a refusal.

Butler, acting as chief prosecutor for the House "managers," emphasized this vital matter in his opening remarks on March 30:

"We claim and respectfully insist that this Tribunal has none of the attributes of a judicial Court as they are commonly received and understood. . . . We suggest, therefore, that we are in the presence of the Senate of the United States convened as a constitutional tribunal, to inquire into and determine whether Andrew Johnson, because of malversation [sic] in office, is longer fit to retain the office of President of the United States. . . . *You are a law unto yourselves, bound only by the natural principles of equity and justice.*" [Italics added.]

This was to be a trial, but it was to be a unique trial, one in which rules of evidence did not apply and principles of law had no place. The issue was settled soon after the Chief Justice of the Supreme Court, Salmon P. Chase, following the dictates of the Constitution, became the presiding officer. He wanted to know whether the Senate was sitting as a court or a legislative body. He preferred the idea that the Senate was a "court of impeachment," but strong expressions of opposition caused him to retreat.

In a further attempt to create a judicial atmosphere, Chase tried to gain authority to pass on the admissibility of evidence, the most sacred power of presiding judges. The Radical Republicans would not hear of it. He would be allowed to rule, but the rule would stand only as long as there was no objection. Should there be one, the Senators would vote the matter up or down.

In order to make sure Chase understood he was an officer of the Senate, the House managers insisted on addressing him as "Mr. President." For his part, ex-Justice Benjamin R. Curtis, Johnson's respected counsel, who had written the dissent in the Dred Scott case, constantly referred to Chase as "Mr. Chief Justice," so that his judicial role would be emphasized.

Curtis underscored his philosophy early in the trial.

"I am here to speak to the Senate of the United States sitting in its judicial capacity as a court of impeachment, presided over by the Chief Justice of the United States, for the trial of the President of the United States. This statement sufficiently characterizes what I have to say. Here party spirit, political schemes, foregone conclusions, outrageous biases can have no fit operation."

Curtis was whistling in the dark. It was precisely in this unique forum that all of those invidious factors were going to play their full, devastating role. The Senators were going to listen to thousands of insistent voices while he spoke, and the loudest ones would be those that spoke to their self-interest and prejudices.

There were no rules to guide them, except for the rules which they made up as they went along. There were no precedents to which they might appeal when faced with a dilemma. This jury of fifty-four had not been screened in any way to insure its impartiality. Twenty-eight Republicans and twelve Democrats among them had screamed out their verdict weeks before the start of the trial. Only fourteen members of the Senate were believed to have somewhat open minds.

The greater majority were for impeachment and they were determined nothing was going to stand in their way. Butler addressed himself to this point immediately: "We define, therefore, an impeachable high crime or misdemeanor to be one in its nature or consequences subversive of some fundamental or essential principle of government, or highly prejudicial to the public interest."

Could anyone listening to him believe Johnson was going to get a fair trial, at least "fair" in the sense commonly given to that word in Anglo-Saxon jurisprudence? The tightly constructed Constitutional language of the impeachment clause was being inflated into a travesty of itself. What did Butler mean by the word "subversive"? Clearly Johnson thought he was incapable of acting subversively.

In addition, Butler's definition of "an impeachable

high crime" as being an act "highly prejudicial to the public interest," left an ambiguous gap in the statutory fence any court would have erected around an accused man.

The truth was that Johnson had entered a pit in which no common murderer would expect to be judged. The post-Civil War Senate contained a high quota of moral defectives. On Johnson's jury were men who had come there by chicanery and others who did not accept the sanctity of the churchbox. Mixed in liberally were honest men, many of whom were confused by a babble of pressuring voices which called out to them from all corners of the country.

And there was no power on earth to whom he could appeal their decision. They were his court of last resort. While he remained quietly in the White House, reading, meditating, entertaining his grandchildren or visiting in the second floor bedroom with his ailing wife, they determined his fate on the basis of their whim.

On May 16, 1868, the Senators had talked themselves out and the issue came to a vote. Article Eleven was considered first. Thirty-six votes were needed for conviction. Stevens was only able to muster thirty-five. Seven Republicans, identified with the more moderate wing of the party, voted for acquittal and their own political oblivion. They were Fessenden of Maine, Fowler of Tennessee, Grimes of Iowa, Henderson of Missouri, Ross of Kansas, Trumbull and Van Winkle of West Virginia. The roll for them deserves to be called. None of them were ever again elected to any political office. A more heroic group of men has never sat in the Senate.

On May 26 another attempt was made to wear down their moral resolve. The second and third articles came before the Senate, but Johnson's supporters held firm, and further attempts at impeachment were dropped. Johnson was allowed to serve out the remaining ten months of his term, but was denied renomination by the vindictive members of his party.

In 1875 Johnson returned to Washington as the newly

elected Senator from Tennessee. Upon entering the Senate chamber he was greeted with cheers and applause and proceeded to shake the hands of all present, some of whom had voted six years earlier to convict him of high crimes and misdemeanors. He did not live out the year, but had lived long enough to witness his complete vindication.

# CHAPTER III

## Crimes That Might Have Led to Impeachment

Andrew Johnson's contemporaries decided the charges against him were of a political nature. This is also the judgment of history. The yardstick of the Constitution called for impeachment for *criminal* acts, yet it was clear that none of Johnson's acts had the slightest taint of criminality.

He was, in short, the prey of politically motivated demagogues, a type which occasionally seizes control of Congress and makes the citizenry tremble for the safety of democratic institutions.

So horrified were Americans at the injustice which had been visited on their President that the very thought of impeaching another chief executive became anathema to them. It was as though the Radical Republicans had by their vicious behavior amended the Constitution to eliminate the possibility of Presidential impeachment.

Thus the clause remained, quiescent, unused, even through the scandals of the Grant administration, when railroad magnates were bribing Congressmen with shares of their stock and gold speculators almost succeeded in cornering the market with the aid of one of the President's relatives.

Part of the reason Grant escaped impeachment was that the practice was out of fashion. But more important, no one believed Grant was anything but a gullible fool. When it came time to accept the resignation of Secretary of War Belknap, Grant held a handkerchief to his eyes to soak up his tears of regret.

No one could accuse Grant of taking part in criminal activity. He was, in fact, its chief victim.

30

Warren Gamaliel Harding's defenders can make the same claim, although perhaps with not as much justice. Harding was a man of weak flesh. Alice Longworth, who knew him well, wrote in her 1934 book, *Crowded Hours,* "Harding was not a bad man. He was just a slob."

This "slob" who was President seems, at this distance, relatively simple-minded. It was not that he had a trusting nature. It was apparently that, in matters concerning ethics and morality, he had only a passing interest. His greatest concern was for voluptuary interludes in the White House bedrooms with Nan Britton, the mistress who bore him a daughter and was indiscreet enough to write a book about it.

Men were hired casually and promoted into his crony cabinet when they demonstrated their ability to lose to him in high stake poker games. It never seemed to have occurred to him some of them might have seen the advantage of losing to him at those moments when he was over-raising most desperately. Mrs. Harding made those occasions congenial by serving bootlegged liquor. The grateful boys referred to her as "Duchess."

However, when he began to understand that his *friends* were accepting bribes from contractors and plungers in quest of leases on government-owned oil lands, he responded with proper indignation. He called the director of the Veterans' Bureau, Charles R. Forbes, to the White House to find out whether he was giving hospital supplies away in return for bribes. Forbes' answers so infuriated Harding that he slammed him against the wall, grabbed him by the throat and cursed him wildly.

As he started off on his ill-fated Alaskan tour, Harding was just beginning to sense the nature of the Teapot Dome scandal, which was to drag through the courts for the next six years. Out in Kansas, as the train chugged over the plains, he confided in William Allen White, editor of the *Emporia Gazette:* "In this job I am not worried about my enemies. I can take care of them. It is my friends who are giving me trouble."

While touring Alaska he heard stories about Interior Secretary Albert Fall's plans to turn public lands over to private exploiters. He wondered aloud to trusted newspapermen what he should do about men who had betrayed him.

On August 2, 1923, while returning from Alaska, Harding suddenly died. Some claimed he had been poisoned by foul crabmeat. He had been lying in bed while Mrs. Harding read aloud a flattering article in the *Saturday Evening Post*.

Before the scandal had run its course several men committed suicide. There seemed grounds to believe that Jess Smith, confidant of the implicated Attorney General Harry Daugherty, a member of the Harding circle, might have been murdered. He is listed by the Washington police as a suicide on May 30, 1923. When the police were finally called to Smith's apartment at the Wardman Park Hotel by Daugherty's friends, they found that Smith had burnt all of Daugherty's household accounts and personal correspondence.

Secretary Fall was tried for bribery over the Teapot Dome leases and sentenced to a year in jail. To him belongs the distinction of being the first Cabinet officer in history to suffer that fate. Forbes was found guilty of conspiracy and served a year and nine months in Leavenworth Penitentiary.

Attorney General Harry Daugherty resigned under pressure and was subsequently tried for conspiring to defraud the government in a matter involving $6,500,-000 in the sale of a German-owned company which had been confiscated during World War I. During the trial he refused to take the stand in his own defense, stating that he could not because of his long, close association with Warren Gamaliel Harding.

There was an implication in Daugherty's remark that Harding's role in the scandals was not completely innocent. Had Daugherty not been such a demonstrable liar, this slander might have received more credit.

What the course of events would have been if Harding had survived can only form the basis of intriguing speculation. At the time of his death he was still an enormously popular man whose administration was thought to be as honest as he was likeable. The full dimensions of the scandal were yet to be revealed, and there was no reason, before his sudden death, to think black thoughts of impeachment.

In the high government scandals in subsequent administrations there was little to warrant the contemplation of that extreme course.

The first sizable scandal after Teapot Dome surfaced during the Truman administration. General Harry H. Vaughan, White House military aide and a personal friend of the President, was guilty of accepting a deep freezer cabinet for services rendered in obtaining special favors. Another Truman aide was involved in the "mink coat" scandals exploited so effectively, and so unfairly, by Richard Nixon in his 1950 California Senatorial campaign against Helen Gahagan Douglas.

In both cases the failure was minor and there was no hint Harry Truman was even involved to the point where he had eaten a steak from the deep freezer, or allowed his wife Bess to run her hand lovingly over the notorious mink.

Although the Republicans in 1952, led by Eisenhower and Nixon, made "corruption" the chief issue of the campaign against Adlai Stevenson, there was only one other instance of Democratic wrongdoing. In 1956, years after Truman had retired to Independence, Missouri, Matthew H. Connelly, Truman's former appointments secretary, was convicted of conspiracy in a matter involving the Internal Revenue Service.

Hard as it may seem to believe, the "golden years" of the Eisenhower administration produced the largest batch of scandals since the time of Harding. Particularly embarrassing to the popular general was that most of the allegations involved *influence peddling,* the major charge he made against the Democrats during his Presidential campaign. In 1955 the Dixon-Yates power scandal gave him months of sleepless nights. Simultaneously there were court actions for bribery and corruption in the letting of garment contracts for Army uniforms. Corruption was also charged in the procurement of airline routes and the issuance of licenses for radio and television stations.

But more serious than any of these, because of the power wielded by the man involved, was the scandal which enmeshed Sherman Adams during Eisenhower's second administration. Adams was commonly referred to as "the Assistant President." Because of his love of hard work, delight over detail, and high sense of responsibility, matched by Eisenhower's love of golf and delight over smiling generalities, Adams was probably, at the time the scandal broke, the most important man in the country.

In early February, 1958, a Congressional committee published letters Adams had written on White House stationery in 1953 urging the Civil Aeronautics Board to postpone a decision its members had made which would have harmed the interests of one of Murray Chotiner's airline clients.

Chotiner was Nixon's campaign manager in 1950 and 1952. Instead of coming to Washington and accepting a low paying, high prestige job in his friend's office, he had set up a lucrative influence peddling practice in the shadow of the White House. Adams had been foolish enough to give Chotiner the appearance of official blessing, which was the minimum required by his harried clients.

Although no one ever claimed Adams exercised this poor judgment for personal gain, a new scandal uncovered by the House Legislative Oversight Committee could not be viewed with the same degree of magnanimity.

It developed that Adams had been allowing a New England textile manufacturer, Bernard Goldfine, to pay hotel and entertainment bills for him for a number of years. Curious investigators quickly discovered that Adams had been making phone calls from the White House for Goldfine, beginning in 1954, to a variety of federal agencies with which the industrialist was having trouble.

As the investigators delved deeper, they discovered that Goldfine had made a series of gifts to his friend adding up, over the years, to several thousand dollars. The gift that caught the public's eye, and started a fashion trend, was a full-length vicuña coat. So popular did they become that for some time the threat of extinction faced the Andean vicuña herds.

Eisenhower was hurt, but Richard Nixon was outraged. He was preparing to run for President against John F. Kennedy and the scandal, he correctly foresaw, might be the margin of his defeat. His maneuverings to get a reluctant Eisenhower to part with Adams' services were unrelenting—and—ultimately responsible for Adams' retirement to New Hampshire.*

Adams did not go to jail, and there is no indication that he ever returned the coat. The fall from power was all the punishment he was ever to receive.

As for Eisenhower, he enjoyed the company of rich men. They received pleasure from giving him expensive additions to his prize Hereford herd on his Gettysburg farm. No one took offense at any of this, for Eisenhower was an extraordinarily popular President to whom few attributed deviousness. Richard Nixon, in his autobiography, *Six Crises,* is the outstanding example of a close associate who was willing to so describe the general. Even if one accepts Nixon's evaluation, deviousness is not considered an impeachable offense.

Lyndon Johnson entered politics as a poor man and left it a millionaire. How he found that golden exit has been described in the press. He received some help from Bobby Baker. On emerging from a seventeen-month prison sentence in 1972, Baker remarked, "I paid my debt," as though to indicate that, now having paid the price, he expected to enjoy the fruits.

Baker's rising fortunes began as he clerked in the

* See *The Running of Richard Nixon;* Coward, McCann & Geoghegan, 1972. Pp. 233-238.

Senate chamber in which his friend Lyndon Johnson sat as a member. A tangle of dealings with lobbyists, businessmen, and political campaign funds, which began surfacing in 1964, brought him a fortune and conviction for larceny, fraud, and tax evasion.

At that time Richard Nixon issued his politically practical version of a moral judgment on President Johnson:

"The people either trust a President all the way or they don't trust him. My observation is that the people's memory of a specific scandal is about three months. . . . But the loss of trust in the President, as a result of the scandal, lingers on."

It says something about contemporary values that, although cries frequently rang out for Johnson's impeachment because of his role in surreptitiously escalating the Vietnam War—a war in which he honestly believed—no similar call was heard because of his dealings with Baker.

For the truth was that impeachment for criminal activity was as out of style as vicuña coats. It was going to take a political earthquake to make Americans turn and look again at the device provided by Washington, Franklin, Adams, and Madison for the protection of democratic institutions against the all too human urge to wield power tyrannically.

# CHAPTER IV

## Nixon's First Brush with Impeachment

Political seismographs detected that earth tremor directly under the Watergate apartment building at two o'clock on the morning of June 17, 1972. At first it did not seem like a major quake, but the shockwaves that followed shook many Washington structures which had seemed secure.

It became apparent, as one looked about in dazed bewilderment, that Richard Milhous Nixon had always been the purveyor of jerry-built structures. To live in a house that he had assembled was a risky matter, and men who did so had always done it at their own peril.

When he burst on the political scene in the 1946 Congressional campaign against the much honored incumbent of the California Twelfth District, Jerry Voorhis, the qualities which were to be most durable were already apparent.

Just out of the navy, he was picked by a group of conservative Republicans who called themselves the Committee of One Hundred to be the sacrificial lamb in a hopeless contest. Since few men volunteer for such a role, the committee had difficulty coming up with a suitable choice. One of its more direct members recalled later, "He was the best of a bad lot."

Nixon's campaign was marked by vilification, obfuscation, smears, and lying. He reached out immediately for the help of Murray Chotiner, who was then a Beverly Hills lawyer specializing in divorce cases. Chotiner had also developed a reputation for being a shrewd campaign manager, a skill not requiring the highest level of probity. Chotiner's advice, repeated to Nixon at many crisis-points in his career, was to take the gloves off and replace them with brass knuckles.

Mild-mannered Voorhis had to be pictured in the voters' minds as the personification of evil. Since our wartime alliance with the Russians was cooling, he had to be represented as a dyed-in-the-wool Communist who was managing to disguise his true Stalinist sentiments only with the greatest difficulty.

Most important, Nixon had to attack, constantly attack, never giving his opponent the opportunity to strike back. He had to make himself an illusive target. He had to speak only in generalities when it came to program, and to brush Voorhis with the most odoriferous tar available.

While Pat handed out leaflets on street corners, bewildered by the sudden change of direction in their six-year marriage, he called Voorhis "a lip-service American." This was his opening sally in a career marked by the imputation of treasonous tendencies to his opponents. He accused Voorhis of "consistently voting the Moscow . . . line in Congress."

Nixon's unexpected victory gave him a seat at age thirty-three in what President Truman was soon to label "the Do-Nothing Republican Congress." However, the young man from Whittier was never one to let grass grow under his feet. Sworn in on January 3, 1947, he was placed on the Education and Labor Committee, which was then working on the Taft-Hartley Act, a piece of anti-union legislation which had been debated heatedly around the country for months.

Since Nixon had informed the press he had come to Washington "to smash the labor bosses," he immediately and furiously involved himself in efforts to finish the committee work and get a tough version of the bill out on the House floor.

As part of his effort, he held a press conference, reported in the *New York Times* of February 17, little more than six weeks after arriving in Washington. He revealed what he claimed to be the results of a number of "grass roots" polls being conducted "individually" on labor matters. "Mr. Nixon asserted that *talks* [italics added] with men in the Scranton, Pa. district indicated a 'unanimous' feeling that 'some legislation was necessary to restrict the power of certain union leaders who overreached themselves and were harming the union movement.'"

There was an immediate uproar, a not uncommon reaction to Nixon's future statements. Who had conducted this "grass roots" poll? How many samples had been taken? What kind of questions had been asked? No one in the Scranton area had seen the freshman Congressman.

The next day Nixon held his first large Washington press conference. As proof of the accuracy of his poll, he read off "excerpts" from some mail he claimed came from Scranton. The writers, he asserted, were union members wanting protection from their leaders. In a righteous voice—which he was always able to muster when under attack—he waved a sheet of paper in the air and then grimly read, "You know these union gangsters will never go for you unless you let them control your vote."

Although in the first *Times* interview he implied he had conducted a full field-study of worker sentiment in the Scranton area, even referring to "talks" in which he had taken part, the first attempts to challenge his assertions caused him to change his story. It was immediately clear that Richard Nixon was not careful with facts, and that when caught in a lie he was capable of producing "evidence."

The fraud involved in this tacky performance was symptomatic of a Nixon trait. Although his supporters maintain he was involved in a trade where such deception was necessary, even common, many politicians go through careers in which their positive work is so pronounced that their occasional human lapses are lost from view. Not so with Richard Nixon. While other freshmen Congressmen were busy finding out what their duties were, he was going off half-cocked. The extreme partisanship and driving ambition which are so much a part of his style were chillingly evident to the reporters who had been taken in by his first story.

The Hiss-Chambers affair, which broke into the head-lines on August 3, 1948, provided an opportunity for the display of Nixon's worst characteristics. Whittaker Chambers, a confessed former Communist who had been out of the Party and working as a magazine editor for approximately ten years, was brought before the House Un-American Activities Committee, on which Nixon sat as a junior member, and accused a former State Department official, Alger Hiss, of once having been a Communist.

That was the substance of his charge. He had made it to the F.B.I. repeatedly through the years. But al-though J. Edgar Hoover was anxious to check out any such allegation of political deviation, his men had never been able to obtain any corroboration. Furthermore, Chambers vehemently denied Hiss had ever taken part in espionage. His total charge was that Hiss had dis-played Communist sympathies during the height of the Depression.

Lacking any confirmation of even these vague charges, the matter languished through the years—that is, until the fateful meeting before J. Parnell Thomas' publicity-seeking, largely discredited committee.

During the executive session at which Chambers first appeared, Nixon reacted negatively to the man who, until his death in 1961, was to be his most intimate friend. "He was short and pudgy," Nixon recalled. "His clothes were unpressed." And the man's story about Communist meetings seemed inconsequential and with-out substance. "Both in appearance and in what he had to say, he made very little impression on me or the other members."

However, the *appearance* of substance was the nec-essary ingredient. The country was swept up in an anti-Communist fever. Mao Tse-tung was about to con-quer China. Thoughts of working cooperatively with him were not to enter Nixon's head for more than twenty years. The Russian's blockade of Berlin, the suppression of democracy in Czechoslovakia, all of these real injustices had enflamed Americans against "subversives" who might be helping our enemies.

The newspapers—then, and until recently, Nixon's greatest ally—gave wide publicity to Chambers' charges. But the suicidal Chambers, who wrote in his auto-biography, *Witness,* that he had tried to take his life three times, once in the midst of the hearings, was not being singled out for newspaper attention. There were a number of Chambers-like figures appearing before private and public groups, partaking in what had be-come a profitable exercise in self-serving confessions.

Quick to detect the publicity potential in Chambers allegations, Nixon rallied to his cause. There was an element of gamble in his decision. The other committee members, in the face of Hiss' forceful denials, had wanted to turn the conflict in testimony over to the Department of Justice and wipe their hands of the con-troversy. His weakness for dramatic plunging was never more clearly delineated than in this sinuous episode.

Under increasing pressure from Nixon over the period of the next three months to come up with new sensa-tions, Chambers nevertheless stuck to his version of the truth. Hiss had been a member of a Communist cell, something like a Marxist study group. This vanguard was to do nothing against Franklin Roosevelt's govern-ment, but was to hold itself in readiness for the coming of the Revolution, which would emerge from the mist of the future within a not easily definable time.

In mid-November, as the balloon was about to col-lapse—a balloon inflated with Chambers hot air and decorated with a lurid picture of a Bolshevik resembling Hiss—Chambers produced some "documents" which he claimed had been sequestered in a dumbwaiter shaft in Brooklyn for over a decade. In an effort to explain why they had not been produced earlier, he claimed to have almost forgotten about them.

The documents proved nothing, although Nixon in-stantly roared that they proved his case. There were sixty-five typewritten pages, some of which had been typed on a machine which, the prosecution stated, had once belonged to Hiss and his wife. Chambers now claimed that the originals of these documents had been removed from the State Department by Hiss, and that *all* of them had then been copied by Mrs. Hiss, on her typewriter, before being given to him for shipment to the Soviet Union.

Suddenly Alger Hiss and his wife Priscilla had become master spies. But in the process Chambers had identified himself as the head of the spy apparatus, a revelation which exposed him to arrest. The documents lent strong support to Chambers' confessions about his own nefarious activities. However, there was nothing to indicate how the documents had come into his possession; he might have picked them out of a wastepaper basket or off the top of a desk on one of the forays he told of making to the State Department building. Therefore, his charges against Hiss still required confirmation.

Chambers was unable to supply that confirmation, and the grand jury seemed to be on the verge of indicting him for crimes he now openly confessed. Convinced that such a catastrophe would destroy his career, since he had allowed Chambers' destiny to become so entwined with his own, Nixon spared no effort to pressure the grand jury. A constant stream of press releases presented Chambers' new allegations as proven facts. The destiny of the Republic would be endangered, Nixon insisted, if Hiss was allowed to continue walking the streets. He personally appeared before the grand jury as it was about to end its months-long deliberations and vote on whether to indict anyone. Supported mightily by the anti-Communist hysteria of the moment, which seemed to permeate the juryroom, Nixon pressured for Hiss's indictment.

Simply because Chambers had repeatedly lied to the F.B.I., to numerous government officials, to the House Un-American Activities Committee, to the grand jury, to the American people, singly and *en masse*, and last, but not least, to Richard Nixon, did not mean he was lying in his final version of the truth. Liars sometimes tell the truth. But to want to send a previously respected man to jail on his word required a monumental suspension of judgment on Nixon's part.

In terms of Nixon, the real lesson to learn was that he had a mental susceptibility which allowed him to convince himself, rapidly and without much evidence, that what he wanted to believe was believable. Furthermore, it showed him capable of pursuing a questionable course without question. Hiss's career was wrecked; his life was left in a shambles. From that wreckage rose the increasingly prominent figure of the future President of the United States.

The Hiss trials laid the foundation for Nixon's 1950 campaign for the Senate from his native state of California. His Democratic opponent was Congresswoman Helen Gahagan Douglas, wife of matinee idol Melvyn Douglas. Superficially the campaign is interesting because of the low level to which Nixon pitched his efforts. It was at this early time that he was pinned with the enduring alias "Tricky Dick," a sobriquet that, significantly, has endured for over a generation. Frequent reference has been made to the fact that he labelled Congresswoman Douglas "the Pink Lady" and distributed Murray Chotiner's "Pink Sheet" that tried to portray her as Stalin's bedmate.

However, in an interview on June 6, 1973, Mrs. Douglas vigorously recalled what was for her the central issue of that campaign.

"He was acceptable to the oil people. He was always against regulating oil drilling. The techniques used (redbaiting and smear tactics) were the least of it. Oil was the big issue. The issue was resources. How were resources going to be used? He had all the money he needed because he favored vested interests of every sort."

Equally significant, however, in terms of the attempts to sabotage the Democratic campaign in 1972, was his elaboration on a technique first tentatively used in the

Voorhis campaign. In 1946 he had urged "true Democrats" not to spend their vote on a man whom he falsely claimed was endorsed by the Communist Party.

By 1950 this appeal to Democrats had taken on a more sinister aspect. In a handbill sent to all registered Democrats he addressed them "As one Democrat to Another." That this was a lie did not deter him. That it succeeded encouraged even more blatant election frauds in the future.

The year 1952 represented the turning point in thirty-nine year old Nixon's career.* The Eastern Establishment cabal, which had guided an aging General Eisenhower to the Republican nomination in Chicago, decided to balance the ticket with a younger man from the West. Nixon had powered his way to the nomination partly with an attack he had launched against Guy Gabrielson, the Chairman of the Republican National Committee.

Although an attack on a leader of his own party seemed gauche, Nixon saw it as an opportunity to assume a moral posture which might counter some of the allegations that he was a man of too easy virtue. He accused Gabrielson of influence peddling in his private legal activities. Although Gabrielson denied he had received any "personal" benefit, Nixon countered relentlessly that a man in his high position, like Caesar's wife, must be above suspicion.

That was a standard Nixon always wanted applied—against his opponents.

In early September, at the beginning of the Presidential campaign, he told an audience in Maine, "If the dry rot of corruption and Communism, which has eaten deep into our body politic during the past seven years, can only be chopped out with a hatchet—then let's call for a hatchet."

That was a particularly inappropriate remark for Nixon to make at that point. He had been deeply involved in advocating the turning over of off-shore oil

* See *The King Makers;* Coward, McCann & Geoghegan: New York, 1971.

acreage to a handful of California and Texas million-aires; and what they returned to him in gratitude was about to be revealed.

On September 18, approximately seven weeks before the election, the *New York Post* printed a story head-lined: SECRET NIXON FUND. The sub-head read, "Secret Rich Men's Trust Fund Keeps Nixon in Style Far Beyond His Salary."

The story that emerged did not make pleasant read-ing. During the previous two years seventy-six individ-uals had been solicited by Murray Chotiner and Nixon finance manager Dana Smith to contribute to a secret fund available only for Nixon's personal use. The funds were deposited in a Pasadena bank under Smith's name. At the time the story broke there were over eighteen thousand pre-inflation dollars in the account. Had not Nixon's nomination as Vice-President made caution ad-visable, the secret, undeclared donations might have continued for years, eventually mounting up to hun-dreds of thousands of dollars.

In a show of bravado, made necessary no doubt be-cause Eisenhower wanted him to resign from the ticket, Nixon told Smith to speak to reporters. That Nixon had not expected the level of frankness Smith subsequently displayed can be assumed from Smith's remarks:

"He [Nixon] told us he needed money. . . . Here we had a fine salesman," which was Smith's quaint way of referring to a United States Senator, "who didn't have enough money to do the kind of selling job we wanted, so we got together and took care of some of those things."

That represented about as tidy a description of the process of bribery as one was likely to hear. Apparently in an effort to prove Nixon an honest man, who gave service for the fee rendered, Smith added: "Dick did just what we wanted him to do."

Through all the sanctimony and tears of the fabled "Checkers" speech, Nixon never stooped to deny a single charge made in the original story. The emphasis, if one can brush aside the sentimental clutter, was on how badly he needed the money, an excuse most felons in state prison would find reasonable.

All eyes were focused on Eisenhower after the speech. How would *he* judge it? What would *he* do? The drama of the moment, and stage directions written in the speech by Nixon, made everyone look in the wrong direction. The common thought was that if the general decided Nixon had done something wrong, then *he* would punish him. And the punishment would be to force his resignation from the ticket.

The general's popularity was so great that assigning him such monarchal discretion did not seem inappropriate. Overlooked by everyone was that Richard Nixon was a United States Senator, and in that capacity was subject to impeachment.

True, there had not been an impeachment of a Senator since the very first impeachment of Blount in 1798. The word impeachment was associated in most minds with the Presidential impeachment of Johnson. However, Senators are "civil officers" of the government, and when they commit a crime while in office—unless they first tender their resignation—they are subject to a trial before their peers.

That Nixon deserved to be impeached is a simple statement of fact. He was guilty of "bribery, high crimes and misdemeanors," if his confession can be taken as proof of guilt. He had violated the conspiracy laws, a high crime, when he plotted with Chotiner and Smith to set up the fund and hid it in a bank under someone else's name. He also violated the income tax law, since he had received income but had not reported it. This was the crime that had placed Al Capone behind bars.

Taken all together, Nixon should not only have been impeached and deprived of his seat; he should have then been tried in a federal court and ended up in Lewisberg prison, perhaps as a cellmate of Alger Hiss. Instead he became Vice-President of the United States, equipped only with the knowledge that steady nerves and the silence one could expect from co-conspirators would see a determined man through.

Is it any wonder that as the years passed he became more concerned with the *image* he projected, and more inclined to find his closest advisors in advertising agencies? If a tale he told on television was able to keep him out of jail and make him Vice-President, then maybe the important thing was not to be honest, but to learn to project the appearance of sincerity.

In an absent-minded way the Congress had neglected its duty and cleared the way for the greater crimes that were to come.

## CHAPTER V

## *How He Played the Game*

As time passed Nixon expanded his reputation as a political hatchet man. He continued to be the cutting edge for Republican campaigns, since this was thought to be his most effective role.

Eisenhower, still smarting over the damage his Vice-President had done to his "Crusade Against Corruption" in 1952, kept him at a distance. He had time enough to socialize with any of the leaders of the top two hundred corporations, but limited the pleasure of the Vice-President's company largely to group gatherings at the weekly Cabinet meetings.

Journalist Ralph de Toledano, who proudly proclaims membership in "the *old* Nixon gang," told a Public Broadcast television audience on October 14, 1971, of the tortured relationship between the country's two leading Republicans:

"He [Nixon] worked for a man [Eisenhower], and I know you shouldn't say this kind of thing—but he worked for a man who in my book was just a complete sadist, and who really cut Nixon to pieces. He would cut him up almost just for the fun of it and I don't think Nixon ever really survived that. I don't think I am talking out of school, and I say that when he was Vice-President and I saw him quite frequently, he would come back from the White House and as much as he ever showed emotion you'd think he was on the verge of tears."

Nixon did everything he could to ingratiate himself with Eisenhower, but his original sin had been just too grievous. Later events wiped out the open hostility—primarily Nixon's Republican nomination in 1960 and the marriage of Eisenhower's grandson David to Nixon's younger daughter Julie. But the early stages of their relationship was a tormenting experience for Nixon, culminating in the humiliation, in 1956, of Eisenhower's attempt to dump him from the second term ticket.

Nixon's most strenuous effort to win over Eisenhower came during the height of Senator Joseph McCarthy's rampage against his own Republican President. By 1953, three years of success at cowing opponents with smears had so emboldened the Wisconsin Senator that he was ready to take on Eisenhower himself.

Instead of fighting back directly, the general enlisted a willing Nixon in a backdoor attempt to compromise. Nixon was the right man for the job, since he had pioneered in character assassination for four years before McCarthy got up in Wheeling, West Virginia, and made his first sally into the field. Even at this point in 1953, when few of his Senatorial colleagues would speak to him, he and Nixon were intimates.

Eisenhower's instructions to Nixon were simple. As Sherman Adams revealed in his book, *First-Hand Report,* he was to tell McCarthy that if he would only confine his attacks to Democrats, there would be no objection from the White House.

That the bargain was not struck cannot be blamed on Nixon. His efforts were prodigious. McCarthy was, by this time, too unrestrained and too unreliable. The end of McCarthy's libelous and divisive activity had to be brought about by his Senatorial colleagues. After a special hearing, akin to a mini-impeachment, McCarthy was officially censured. This 1954 resolution brought about his immediate disgrace and the end of his power.

The Senate, although unwilling to go to impeachment, had accepted its responsibility. Had McCarthy's health not been on the decline, ending in his death in 1957, an aroused Senate, under continued provocation, might eventually have employed this ultimate weapon.

In all of this turmoil, Nixon was the one "top administration spokesman" with whom the Wisconsin Senator was willing to deal. A sign of McCarthy's appreciation for his efforts came on the day he was buried. Nixon was one of his honorary pallbearers.

One either liked or disliked the political positions Richard Nixon adopted during the decade from 1952 to 1962. The Nixon of that time approved. The post-1968 Nixon disapproved. Most clearly to the distaste of the later-day Nixon would be the remark he made to the American Society of Newspaper Editors on April 18, 1954, concerning the French effort in the Vietnam war. At that time we were not yet involved.

"The United States as a leader of the free world cannot afford further retreat in Asia. . . . If France stops fighting in Indo-China and the situation demands it, the United States will have to send troops to prevent the Communists from taking over this gateway to Southeast Asia."

Time has tended to obscure the fact that Nixon was among the earliest and most consistent advocates of escalating American military participation in Southeast Asia. His reluctance to end the war rapidly after his 1968 election, as he had promised in the campaign, can perhaps be attributed to the unswerving philosophy revealed in his 1954 remark: "We have learned that if you are weak and indecisive, you invite war. You don't keep Communists out of an area by telling them you won't do anything to save it."

Even that resolve changed under the pressure of the 1972 Presidential race.

One of the most outstanding revelations of Nixon's plastic morality under the pressure of political campaigning came in 1954. Eisenhower, by then devoting increasing amounts of time to sharpening his game on the putting green he had installed on the White House lawn, placed Nixon in charge of speaking for Republicans running in the Congressional off-year elections.

Once again Nixon went beyond the bounds of propriety. For two months he criss-crossed the country waving the silken lining of the Truman mink coat. He alternated discussion of this "issue" with dozens of speeches in which implications of treason were buried not far beneath the surface. Typical of these was his oration at a rally in Rock Island, Illinois, on October 21:

"The President's security risk program resulted in 6,926 individuals removed from the federal service. . . . The great majority of these individuals were inherited largely from the Truman regime. . . . Included in this number were individuals who were members of the Communist Party and Communist-controlled organizations."

In Denver on November 1, he made the charge more specific and more inaccurate. "96 per cent of the 6,926 Communists, fellow-travelers, sex perverts, people with criminal records, dope addicts, drunks, and other security risks removed under the Eisenhower security program were hired by the Truman administration."

The figures were impressive, but bogus. Eisenhower's chairman of the Civil Service Commission, Philip Young, issued a denial, *after the election,* stating he did not know of a single person who had been fired by the Eisenhower Administration for being a Communist or fellow-traveller.

Months later he issued an analysis of the *3,746* government workers who had been dismissed, or had resigned, between May, 1953, and mid-1955, after being *accused* of being *possible* security risks. Almost every one of them was an alleged homosexual or alcoholic. Contrary to Nixon's assertions, 41.2 per cent had been hired by the Eisenhower administration.

To this point in his career, Nixon had contributed nothing but discord to the political scene. Although he had served four years in the House of Representatives and two years in the Senate, there was not a single piece of legislation which bore his name. As in the case of most of the rest of his career, his major interest seemed to be in advancing his prospects, and his most dedicated supporter would find it difficult to point to one positive contribution he had made before entering the White House in 1969.

However, lack of accomplishments and lack of knowledge never deterred him. In 1957, on the eve of being inaugurated for a second time as Vice-President, he gave an interview to the *New York Times*. In a mood approaching euphoria, the forty-four year old Nixon guilelessly admitted, "Looking back, my knowledge of world problems four years ago was pretty much limited. . . ."

It was a strange confession from a man who had accepted a nomination four years earlier to an office which might at any moment place him in charge of American foreign policy. The fact that he was "pretty much limited," and poorly equipped to handle the job, did not keep him from wanting it.

Having apparently learned what foreign policy was all about in the intervening four years, Nixon devoted his speeches on the subject to aggressive anti-Communism, with emphasis on the need to "liberate" areas under Communist rule. The fact that his was a sure formula for starting World War III did not deter him.

His belligerence showed through dramatically in the controversy over two tiny islands, Quemoy and Matsu, situated three miles off the coast of Communist China. These islands, so small they appear only on the most detailed local maps of that area, were in the hands of Chiang Kai-shek's Nationalist army. In 1958 Mao began lining up his forces to seize them. Nixon responded loudly, stating that he opposed the policy of "appeasement." The time had come to end the ten year old regime of the Chinese Communists and return Chiang to the mainland.

However, the American people did not agree. At this point an incident occurred which is reminiscent of one in May of 1972—when Ronald Zeigler released doctored results on American reaction to Nixon's decision to mine Haiphong Harbor.

On September 27, 1958, the *Times* reported that eighty per cent of the mail received by the State Department opposed the Eisenhower-Nixon determination to fight for the two off-shore islands. Unlike press secretary Zeigler's manipulated count, which was released to give a false picture of popular support for President Nixon's 1972 action, the *Times* report was accurate.

Nixon lashed out at the anonymous "subordinate" who had tried to "sabotage" the President's Quemoy-Matsu policy by disclosing the negative count.

In 1972 the same problem was handled with greater finesse. A flood of telegrams was sent to Zeigler's office *sub rosa* by the Committee for the Re-election of the President. These telegrams congratulated Nixon for his courage in doing what Goldwater had been proposing since 1964. The result was a tally against which the President did not have to aim any denunciations.

By 1959 Nixon was concentrating all his efforts on the 1960 Presidential campaign. Eisenhower had been such a star during his eight years as President that few candidates had developed as possible successors. The limelight had shone too brightly on him. Nixon was the chief beneficiary of this inability of potential candidates to thrive in Eisenhower's shadow. Sick and weary since 1955, when he had suffered a major heart attack and later undergone stomach surgery, Eisenhower could not summon the energy necessary to oppose Nixon's nomination.

Winning the nomination and winning the election are two different things. 1960 was not Nixon's year. He lost by the slenderest of margins, scarcely 133,000 out of 68,800,000 votes cast. But trying hard and coming close was no consolation to him. He said, "I have never had much sympathy for the point of view, 'It isn't whether you win or lose that counts, but how you play the game.' "

Part of the reason Nixon lost in 1960 can be traced back to another personal scandal which began in 1956, but which was first spoken about during his contest with Kennedy.

Although one would imagine that after the 1952 fund scandal Nixon would have avoided even the semblance of dishonesty, he involved himself in another odoriferous deal in 1956, being discreet enough only to activate it after the election.

His brother Donald, one of two younger brothers still alive, had been trying to make his fortune by establishing a chain of restaurants in Southern California. By late 1956 the operation was losing $5,600 a week. He needed a loan.

Why millionaire Howard Hughes should have had any interest in rescuing Donald from bankruptcy has never been explained. Did the fact that his brother was Vice-President influence him in any way? Also unrevealed was who requested the loan.

All that is known for certain is this: although Donald Nixon of Whittier did not know Howard Hughes of Las Vegas, the country's tenth largest government contractor nonetheless decided in December, 1956, to lend $165,000 to him. Several months later, when it was obvious he was throwing good money after bad, he upped the ante $40,000.

Giving the deal an air of criminality was the method used by Hughes to disguise his largess. He first had the funds transferred to Frank J. Waters, an attorney for Hughes Tool Company. Mr. Hughes books showed only that this was a loan to Mr. Waters. Why the deception?

Shortly after the second injection of Hughes money, Donald's restaurants were declared bankrupt. Since part of the loan had been secured by a lien on a vacant Whittier lot owned by Hannah Nixon, Hughes was able to salvage about a quarter of his "investment."

However, so intent was he on hiding his connection to the Nixon family that he had Donald's mother turn over her forfeited lot to Phillip Reiner, an accountant working with Mr. Water's law partner.

Mr. Reiner kept his peace for several years, but as the 1960 Presidential campaign approached and word of the loan began to leak out, he apparently decided he was not going to become the scapegoat in the mushrooming scandal.

The F.B.I. began to probe the affair soon after Kennedy was elected, and Reiner hired criminal lawyer Melvin Belli to protect his interests. Belli aggressively filed a damage suit against Hughes, claiming his client "had been made to appear as the lender of the money so that any inquiry would lead to him and stop, shielding Mr. Hughes and the tool company."

Reiner insisted he "had been deceived in the role he played" and said Hughes had "intentionally and fraudulently concealed" from him "the true nature of their dealings with the Nixon family."

Hughes instructed his attorney to settle out of court, asking only that Reiner and Belli pledge not to discuss what had happened. It was not until January 23, 1972, approximately when the wiretapping of Democratic headquarters was being discussed by Attorney General John Mitchell and his confederates, that the *New York Times* printed the details of the transaction.

From a ten year old Department of Justice file which had come into the "possession" of the *Times,* it was discovered that then Attorney General Robert F. Kennedy had given "serious thought" to indicting the Nixons under statutes governing political contributions. He also considered the possibility of charging Hughes with offering a bribe, which logically suggested—although the *Times* did not—that he must have considered charging someone with *accepting* a bribe.

The *Times* added, "Income tax consequences were examined for the Nixon family and none were found worth considering."

It was not that income tax *consequences* had not been found; the Attorney General merely decided, after his brother's recent victory over Richard Nixon, that further action against the Nixons was not "worth considering."

What stayed the Justice Department from seeking indictments against the Nixons on bribery charges and violations of the income tax laws is a matter of conjecture. That Richard Nixon had once again brushed up against the law was suggested, but not as incontestably proven as was his felonious involvement with the 1952 Pasadena slush fund. In both cases thoughts of putting him in jail were brushed aside by men concerned with personal problems.

If Phillip Reiner had been forced to repeat his testimony before a grand jury, and if Frank Waters, Howard Hughes, Donald Nixon and his mother had been asked to explain their actions under oath in the light of Reiner's assertions, there is little doubt but that Richard Nixon's career would have been ruined.

Instead the matter was hushed up and Nixon emerged from the 1960 Presidential contest with a stronger standing than ever in the Republican party. It was obvious he could not be denied the nomination in 1964 if he wanted it.

However, he decided he first wanted to be governor of California. It was in pursuit of that minor office, a pursuit seemingly motivated by nothing more than a nervous man's desire to keep moving, that the ugly story of Howard Hughes' donation to Donald Nixon's welfare was converted into a central campaign issue.

The fact that Bobby Kennedy had been considering criminal action never came to light. Still, the zigzag windings of this grubby transaction placed Nixon constantly on the defensive.

As it became apparent he might lose, his instinct to win at any price took control. In an episode similar to the 1972 Republican effort to sabotage the Democratic Presidential campaign, the most insidious outlines of the future strategy were fully discernible. Even the cast of characters was similar. Herbert W. Kalmbach, destined to be Nixon's personal attorney as the Watergate scandal broke, and John D. Ehrlichman, who was in charge of much of the Watergate cover-up attempt, were both active.

Nixon's campaign manager that year was H. R. Haldeman, a young advertising man from the J. Walter Thompson agency. Haldeman had been working in various lowly capacities in Nixon campaigns going back to 1952. However, he had never held a more important position than *advance man*. In that capacity he set up the schedules for his candidate, arranged hotel reservations, and rented the car to get Nixon from the airport to the place where he'd deliver his speech.

Murray Chotiner would have been the obvious choice to run a California Nixon campaign. However, his influence peddling disgrace before the Senate investigating committee in 1956 made that choice impractical. So while Chotiner came in through the back door to advise his faithful friend, Haldeman took public charge of the campaign.

Driven to desperation by the thought the campaign might prove to be a disaster, Haldeman and Nixon decided to use sabotage against their opponent, the not-too-popular incumbant governor Edmund G. "Pat" Brown. They took $70,000 out of the huge kitty donated to the Nixon for Governor Committee and fed it to a cover organization called the Committee for the Preservation of the Democratic Party (CPDP).

From the first the CPDP was a Republican Party organ. From the same instant it represented itself as an instrument of the Democratic Party. The $70,000 was to be used for only one purpose. It was to finance a "postcard poll" to 900,000 conservative registered Democrats. At the proper moment the results of the poll were published. The covering lie on the report of the fragmented results was that it represented the "voice of the rank and file Democrats."

According to Nixon's pollsters, the results proved Democrats were concerned about the welfare of their party. They were pictured as feeling that, unless Nixon was elected, the California Democratic Party would be destroyed.

The Democratic State Committee went to court seeking an injunction to halt the operations of the CPDP, whose only avowed purpose was the "Preservation of the Democratic Party."

The case was heard before Superior Court Judge Byron Arnold in San Francisco. After two years of wrangling, long after the important issue had been settled at the polling booths, Judge Arnold signed a stipulated judgment declaring the poll was fraudulently conceived and executed.

The action of the CPDP was misleading, Judge

Arnold ruled, because it failed to disclose the mailing was supported and financed by the Nixon for Governor Finance Committee. He also ruled that the committee had passed itself off as fearing the destruction of the Democratic Party when, in reality, nothing could have pleased it more. Then, turning in the direction of the future President of the United States, Judge Arnold noted that the postcard poll was "revised, amended and finally approved by Mr. Nixon personally."

This was no case of a man above the battle unaware of what his "overzealous" supporters were doing. He not only knew about it—he was ordering their every move.

The judge did not ignore Haldeman. He noted in the record that Nixon's future major-domo in the White House had known of the meretricious nature of the poll, yet had approved its mailing.

There were several aspects of state and federal law clearly violated. There had been a conspiracy by Nixon and Haldeman to defraud the Democratic voters of California. They were trying to obstruct the honest conduct of an election. Furthermore, it must be presumed the people who donated the $70,000 to what they believed was a legitimate, traditional political campaign would never have done so if they thought the money was going to be used illegally.

Why was Nixon allowed to go scot free, only having to pay a wrist slapping $100 to the Democratic State Central Committee and an assessment of $268.50 in court costs? Part of the answer was that people in California, who knew Nixon best, expected this type of behavior from him. There was no sense of shock over something new. He had been misbehaving for years.

Furthermore, it seemed relatively petty. True, it was an escalation of the Helen Gahagan Douglas campaign lie, "As one Democrat to Another," but it was still a long way from the massive sabotage and espionage efforts of the 1972 campaign.

Perhaps more important than any of this, Nixon lost, and lost badly. His margin of defeat in California was three times greater than what it had been in his 1960 national campaign. And he had acted disgracefully in defeat, berating the reporters, as he announced his concession to Brown, for writing "slanted" stories against him and being the major cause of his defeat.

Near the end of his fifteen-minute, often incoherent diatribe, he said: "Just think how much you're going to be missing. You won't have Nixon to kick around any more because, gentlemen, this is my last press conference and it will be one in which I have welcomed the opportunity to test wits with you."

Murray Chotiner, who had been upstairs watching Nixon's perspiring face on television, said, "Let's face it. He was through. He thought he was finished in politics and he was right."

That was the opinion of most Californians. If the man was finished, why pursue him? Hadn't he suffered a fall from a great enough height? What purpose would it serve to find him guilty of distributing sneaky postcards? Allow him the peace of his well-earned obscurity.

*Time* Magazine, in its next issue, remarked: "Barring a miracle, Nixon's political career has ended."

Overlooked in this forecast was that often the only way for a person to become President of the United States is for him to be the beneficiary of scores of miracles. The selection process is that chancey, and survival that uncertain.

Had Nixon been adequately punished for the mischief he and Haldeman performed in the 1962 campaign, the nation would have been spared the convoluted criminality on the highest level that it now faces.

# CHAPTER VI

## *The Years in the Wilderness*

For the next six years Nixon was a private citizen, primarily concerned with building a fortune. He became a senior partner in the prestigious New York law firm of Mudge, Rose, Guthrie and Alexander. At his side during this period was the future Attorney General, John Mitchell, also a senior partner. Leonard Garment, a brilliant lawyer from Brooklyn, was in charge of litigation. His morale rebuilding services were so instrumental in putting Nixon's bruised ego back together that in May, 1973, when Watergate was threatening an even more soul-searing impact on the President, he was sworn in as White House chief counsel.

On the eve of his second inauguration, December 20, 1972, President Nixon spoke of those years to a *Times* reporter. "I'd been through enough [before becoming President]—those shattering defeats in 1960 and 1962, and then those eight years in the wilderness."

In 1964 Nixon began to suspect he had not reached the end of the political trail. Barry Goldwater was selected by the Republicans to be their candidate against then popular Lyndon Johnson, who had become President on November 22, 1963, when John Kennedy was assassinated.

Nixon rallied to the cause of conservative Goldwater, but almost immediately found he and the Arizona Senator were out on the limb by themselves. The election, much as in the case of the George McGovern race in 1972, seemed to be decided at the convention. Goldwater stood before the television cameras with a glint of determination in his eyes as he delivered his acceptance speech saying "extremism in defense of liberty is no vice," and "moderation in the pursuit of justice is no virtue."

This might well have been Nixon's admonition to his staff as they were plotting the wiretapping of his 1972 Democratic opponents. That he was not repelled by the anti-democratic philosophic overtones of Goldwater's remarks is demonstrated by the active role he played in the increasingly hopeless campaign. While most other Republican leaders sat on their hands, a few even going so far as to endorse Goldwater's opponent, Nixon raced around the country, campaigning as compulsively as if he were the candidate.

Murray Chotiner sat with me in his law office in the summer of 1971 as the Watergate burglers, G. Gordon Liddy and E. Howard Hunt, Jr., were first being hired across the street by the White House, and proudly explained why Nixon's strenuous efforts in an obviously hopeless cause had been the wisest use of his energies. "After Goldwater's defeat, it was clear that Dick was going to be the party nominee in 1968. He had more brownie points than anyone."

And so it was that, when the Republicans met in Miami in 1968, Nixon was the recipient of Goldwater's grateful support and won the nomination without difficulty. However, winning the election was not as easy. He had not, in fact, won an election on his own since defeating Helen Gahagan Douglas in 1950, and seemed to have permanently lost the knack.

The decision was to turn the campaign over to the agency men. He agreed to be sold as any other commodity in the market place. First the packaging had to be right. An American flag was always pinned in the lapel, as though this established his monopoly over the title *patriot*. Then the advertising theme had to be approved. What better slogan than "law and order"? How meaningless a slogan it was became apparent after he assumed office. The national crime statistics rose in excess of ten per cent each of his first three years, and in his own private conduct of the Presidency he condoned the employment of criminality. The vital consideration was to find the selling key and then use it. Vietnam, the most important issue of the day, was to be avoided as if it did not exist.

How to *present* the advertising campaign was a major problem. Normally candidates are verbal and so well-rehearsed, so inured to crowds and, often, so pleased to have large numbers of people listen to them that touring the hustings is a pleasant experience for them. Not so with Nixon—especially after the four disastrous televised debates with John F. Kennedy in 1960.

By nature an introvert (the members of his family often speak of his "shyness"), never at ease before large groups, Nixon found public speaking to be an increasingly painful experience. That he drove himself to it is a measure both of his determination and his willingness to endure great suffering in order to prevail.

The advertising men about him had, along with John Mitchell, taken complete charge of the campaign. They admired his unyielding resolution, but they were confronted with the fact that he was an increasingly inept campaigner.

There was nothing appealing about his platform style. As he spoke, it sounded as if he were trying to recall what the next line was in his memorized routine. And the clenched fist, with which he emphasized each monumentally irrelevant point, often seemed like it was being waved as a threat at his audience. The image he projected at those times of public display was perhaps best summed up by the question under the famous picture of an over-radiant Nixon with a fixed smile: "Would you buy a used car from this man?"

There was no profit in taking a chance. Most of Nixon's campaign money—and $35,000,000 was collected in what was until 1972 the most expensive of all campaigns—went into canned commercials, filmed after extensive rehearsals, and edited with a professional touch possessed only by men who had made a career of selling cigarettes and other shoddy products to the gullible.

Despite the extraordinary caution and unlimited expenditure of money, Nixon was almost defeated. During the last three weeks of the campaign, Hubert H. Humphrey, ebullient, quick-witted and honest, came on with a rush. His most serious liability had been the fact that he was Vice-President under an increasingly unpopular Lyndon Johnson. But as election day approached, the prospect of Nixon as President had disturbed enough traditional Democrats so that the canvasses showed the original gap between the two candidates was narrowing rapidly.

The projection of the daily polls during the last week indicated that, if the campaign had gone three more days, Humphrey would have won. A 19 per cent advantage for Nixon in August, ended as a 43.4 to 42.7 per cent squeaker.

This was one of the most enduring results of the 1968 contest. The nearness of yet another defeat so impressed itself on the minds of Nixon and his staff that it called for *special* plans to insure that the same thing, or even worse, would not happen in the 1972 reelection fight.

Humphrey's dramatic last minute gains had shattered the confidence of the men around Nixon, and convinced the President-elect that his last campaign for office in 1972 was going to have to be waged as aggressively as any he had ever fought.

Contributing to the pessimism about 1972 was the course of events after he was sworn-in at the beginning of 1969. He had been inaugurated at a time of unsurpassed prosperity. Real national income had grown 50 per cent in the eight years since he had been Vice-President. Unemployment was at 3.3 per cent, a near-record low. Furthermore, between 1965, when Johnson began to pour larger quantities of money into the escalating military effort in Vietnam, and election day 1968, the annual inflation rate had remained a steady, relatively moderate 2.5 per cent.

Nixon's spot commercials had pictured the 2.5 per cent figure as being excessive—in fact, a runaway inflation. On assuming office, he began applying traditional Republican economic nostrums to lower that rate. Instead, by the end of his first year in office, the inflation rate was 5 per cent. Within the next twelve months it rose to the frightening rate of 6 per cent.

The decline in his popularity was also caused by his unwillingness to end America's involvement in the Vietnam war and bring home our prisoners of war, as he had promised. In fact, during the first year of his tenure, additional troops were sent to Southeast Asia as he made an expensive effort to overwhelm the North Vietnamese.

The national debt rose astronomically. Each year he was in office the budget deficit of the previous year was exceeded. The same bad news surrounded our negative balance of payments in trade with the rest of the world. The American dollar had to be devalued twice, and the real value of the dollar, in terms of what it could buy at home, declined sharply.

His reaction to all of this was to build a bureaucratic wall around him that kept out messengers bearing bad news and gave him the feeling of tranquillity in the midst of the plunging indicators.

During the Eisenhower years, Nixon had his Vice-Presidential offices in the Executive Office Building, a short distance from the White House. Unaccountably, he had an office set up there after he was inaugurated, where he spent most of his work-day on the infrequent occasions when he was in Washington. He referred to this as "the Quiet Room."

Harry Truman had been forced to set up offices in the Blair House, across Pennsylvania Avenue, while the White House was remodeled, but no other President had voluntarily sought such a hidden den outside the Oval Room. No other President, with the possible exception of Calvin Coolidge, had been such a private person, so anxious to avoid contact with people, so determined to arrange matters through intermediaries.

The press conference, which had been a major Presidential instrument for conveying information to the public, and, at the same time one of the chief sources of information for the President, fell into disuse. Eisenhower, while healthy, faced a half hour press conference once a week. Nixon never held more than nine press conferences during any of the four years of his first term.

There were no compensating mechanisms created to keep the President informed. Antiseptic news summaries, prepared by Haldeman, further cut him off from sources of information. Except for viewing of sports events, he avoided television, having an absolute phobia about looking at himself on film.

In the 1972 pre-inauguration *Times* interview, he discussed his emotional response to television.

"This office as presently furnished probably would drive President Johnson up the wall. He liked things going on. He kept three TV sets here. I have none here or in my bedroom. . . .

"I could go up the wall watching TV commentators. I don't. I get my news from the news summary the staff prepares every day and it's great; it gives all sides.

"I never watch TV commentators or the news shows when they are about me. That's because I don't want decisions influenced by personal emotional reactions."

Within a short time of assuming office, Nixon had set up a staff structure which was so impenetrable that access to the President was less possible than it had been for any occupant of that office in American history.

Harry Robbins ("Bob") Haldeman became chief of staff. The crew cut, unsmiling Haldeman was born in Los Angeles on October 27, 1926, into an upper middle class family. His father ran a pipe and building supply company inherited from his grandfather, who had been one of the founders of the Better American Foundation, an early anti-Communist organization. He earned a degree in business administration at UCLA.

It was at UCLA that he met John Ehrlichman, who had lived in Tacoma, Washington, before his family moved to Southern California. The two roomed together at college, but afterward Ehrlichman went on to establish a law practice in Seattle, specializing in zoning and land development, while Haldeman applied what he had learned in business administration to the handling of advertising accounts for Walt Disney, 7-Up and Black Flag Insect Spray.

In 1970, already the second most important man in Nixon's government, Haldeman expressed his regal viewpoint in a rare interview:

"I want to make sure we don't enforce a common level of mediocrity by putting through programs that tend to lower everybody to a standard which can be attained by the majority."

Haldeman was in a position to impress his views on policy matters. He had surrounded the President's office with men whose first loyalty was to him. Dwight L. Chapin, who became Nixon's appointments secretary, had worked for Haldeman at the J. Walter Thompson agency in Los Angeles. Jeb Stuart Magruder and Gordon Strachan, both Presidential assistants, had been hired by Haldeman.

Nixon's former press secretary Herbert Klein was given the grand title Director of Communication and assigned an office away from the White House. Sitting at the White House Press Secretary's desk was Ronald Zeigler, 29, another Haldeman/J. Walter Thompson protégé.

Even faithful Rose Mary Woods, who had run Nixon's offices for him through fat and lean times, was shunted to quarters far enough from her boss's desk so that she lost the privilege of informal contact with him.

When an outsider like Murray Chotiner was added to the staff as a sentimental gesture by Nixon at the beginning of 1969, it only took nine months for the new "White House General Counsel" to understand he was not welcome.

Haldeman's control was so complete he was able to frustrate Leonard Garment's desire to be appointed as Nixon's chief legal counsel, and instead filled that position with thirty-one year old John Wesley Dean III.

Haldeman's real source of power was his ability to determine who would see the President, and what memorandum would be placed before his eyes. Within a short time he was able to brag, "Even Mitchell comes through me."

All the evidence indicates that this was what Richard Nixon wanted. He had yearned to be President for almost two decades; and now that he was, he yearned most for the serenity of Key Biscayne, Grand Cay, San Clemente, Camp David or the "Quiet Room," where disturbing influences could be strained out by loyal Bob. The crises, the conflicts, were now in the past. He was President of the United States.

# CHAPTER VII

## The First Criminal Activity

There were signs as early as mid-1969 that the men working for Nixon were not sufficiently concerned with traditional concepts of American democracy. In this lack of concern were planted the seeds of the Watergate weed.

As the President's popularity declined sharply, he became increasingly concerned about leaks which were flowing from high administration sources to certain newsmen. He demanded to know how newspapermen were finding out about policy discussions taking place within the government.

The President first asked that the FBI tap the telephones of William Beecher and Hedrick Smith, both of the *New York Times,* and Henry Brandon, Washington correspondent for the *Sunday Times* of London. Subsequently the requested number was raised to six, when reporters for the *Washington Post* were added.

J. Edgar Hoover, director of the FBI for forty years, found the request disturbing. He balked, informing the President that the practice would be indefensible if discovered. He finally agreed to install the taps, but only if directed to do so in writing by his immediate superior in the Justice Department, Attorney General Mitchell.

Never one to cavil at details, Mitchell affixed his signature to the order, giving as his reason the need for domestic "security." He thereby believed he had avoided the necessity of getting a court order for each tap. At the same time the net was cast wider, and the phones of seventeen newsmen and White House aides were monitored.

In this manner, the phone of Dr. Morton Halperin, member of the National Security Council, was bugged;

and the Justice Department later revealed that Daniel Ellsberg was overheard using this phone in late 1969 and early 1970. This was more than a year and a half before his notoriety over the Pentagon Papers. The inability of the FBI to produce copies of these conversations, after it had revealed existence of the taps—the substance of which conversations may have been used in preparing the prosecution against Ellsberg—contributed to Judge William Byrne's decision to throw the government's two million dollar case out of court on May 11, 1973.

It was three days after the mistrial had been declared that FBI agents, smarting over the disgrace which the White House had inflicted on the agency's previously good reputation, uncovered the seventeen tap records in the office safe of John Ehrlichman. Nixon's assistant, who had resigned two weeks earlier, had allowed the government's case to be destroyed sooner than admit he had possession of them. Ehrlichman was apparently guilty of obstruction of justice.

This type of broadgauged surveillance continued for two years, and was approved again by L. Patrick Gray, the acting director of the FBI appointed by Nixon after Hoover's death in May, 1972. It ended only when the Supreme Court, this time weighted with four conservative Nixon appointees, declared the practice of *domestic* wiretapping in security cases, without a court order, unconstitutional.

However, even before the Supreme Court ruled, Hoover had become increasingly irascible toward his Justice Department superiors, and Mitchell moved to pressure him into resigning. Deputy Attorney General Richard Kleindienst even went so far as to publicly suggest it was time for Congress to investigate the FBI.

Although close to death, Hoover retained his fighting instincts. He phoned Kleindienst and threatened to reveal that Nixon had ordered the phones of newspapermen tapped as far back as May 9, 1969. Since this was a possible violation of the First Amendment of the Constitution, which guaranteed freedom of the press, and since the taps themselves were probably illegal, lacking the authorization of a court order, Hoover's threat had to be taken seriously.

On May 14, 1973, William C. Sullivan, former FBI assistant director, revealed why Nixon, Mitchell, and Kleindienst might have grown uneasy with Hoover. "Hoover wasn't of sound mind," Sullivan told the *Los Angeles Times*. "As a matter of fact a high Administration official once said Hoover had been of unsound mind for the past few years. Everybody who had anything to do with Hoover knew that he was no longer rational."

If true, it meant that Hoover's superiors had allowed him to remain in charge of "the nation's police force" when he should have been under medical attention.

Sullivan had voiced his opposition to Hoover many times during the last four years. "That fellow was a master blackmailer and he did it with considerable finesse despite the deterioration of his mind."

At the time of his statement Sullivan was director of the Justice Department's Office of National Narcotics Intelligence. He described what he claimed was Hoover's technique:

"The moment he would get something on a Senator he'd send one of the errand boys up and advise the Senator that we're in the course of an investigation and we by chance happened to come up with this data on your daughter. But we wanted you to know this—we realize you'd want to know it. But don't have any concern, no one will ever learn about it. Well, Jesus, what does that tell the Senator? From that time on the Senator's right in his pocket."

One does not like to think that *The FBI In Peace and War* had to stoop to that level of intrigue in order to retain J. Edgar Hoover on the job. But the old man's threats were making the White House tense. Something had to be done to remove the club that was hanging over the President's head.

In mid-1971, while FBI agents still had their earphones on, Hoover discovered all of his records on the taps had disappeared. An intense in-house investigation

was begun. Sullivan was pinpointed and forced to resign on October 6, 1971.

Hoover's right-hand man, W. Mark Felt, then traced
the documents to Robert C. Mardian, at that time an
Assistant Attorney General, soon to be involved in the
machinations of the Committee for the Reelection of
the President. He approached Mardian and asked him
if he knew who had the documents. His curt answer:
"Ask the President. Or ask Mitchell."

The implication of Mardian's remarks were unpleasant. They suggested the President of the United States
had ordered an action against a law enforcement agency
of the federal government. Undoubtedly the removal of
the files did not seem that sinister to Sullivan, Mardian,
Mitchell or the President. It was simply a matter of
taking something from a government file that the head
of the government wanted. However, they knew Hoover
had no intention of letting those documents out of his
hands, and the only way to get it from him was by some
sort of foul-play. John Ehrlichman's White House safe
was apparently the correct place to conceal the results
of that foul play.

That two years of snooping did not result in uncovering the source of the *New York Times* information
merely raised Nixon's sense of indignation. During the
summer of 1971 he ordered an intensification in the
efforts when matters pertaining to U.S.-Soviet Strategic
Arms Limitation Talks (SALT) began to appear in
that paper.

Those middle months of 1971 were an exceedingly
difficult time for him. Inflation was getting out of hand.
Unemployment was at 6 per cent. The balance of payments reports were among the worst in the nation's
history. In May the Harris poll indicated he was trailing
the probable Democratic Presidential nominee, Edmund
Muskie of Maine, by eight points.

On August 15 he was going to have to announce
"Phase I" wage and price controls, a Democratic approach to economics he had pledged never to use.

On June 13, in the midst of these difficulties, Daniel

Ellsberg released the Pentagon's unexpurgated history of the Vietnam war to the *New York Times*.

Nixon was furious. Charles Colson recalls attending White House meetings in July at which the Pentagon Papers were being discussed, and describes them as "kind of panic sessions."

Nixon ordered Mitchell to plug the leaks of information within two weeks. Mitchell realized no matter how badly Nixon wanted the leaks stopped, it would be foolish to ask Hoover to tap additional phones in this cause. The FBI director was still seething over the disappearance of his files.

However, Nixon's anger left Mitchell no alternative. White House aides were instructed to set up their own spy operation. Although it had connections with the Justice Department, so sensitive were these operations that they completely bypassed the FBI and were centered within the White House. John Ehrlichman was put in charge.

It was at this point that G. Gordon Liddy and E. Howard Hunt, Jr., were recruited into the White House staff and the Watergate team began to be assembled.

# CHAPTER VIII

## The Plumbers' First Job

Egil Krogh, then deputy assistant for domestic affairs on Ehrlichman's staff, recommended Liddy. Charles W. Colson, special counsel to the President, and Ehrlichman's most trusted assistant, recommended Hunt, a personal friend of his for many years.

Both men were interviewed by Ehrlichman for final approval. Colson recalls receiving a call from Ehrlichman, then in California with the President, directing him to put Hunt to work.

General Robert E. Cushman, deputy director of the CIA, was called July 3, 1971, from the White House and told Hunt had been hired for a national security investigation. Cushman was urged to make sure Hunt received the agency's cooperation.

G. Gordon Liddy, a flamboyant, cigar-smoking extrovert, who was to become the field commander of the elaborate spy apparatus, was born in New York City on November 30, 1930. After service in the Korean War, he went back to Fordham for his law degree. He worked for the FBI in the late 1950's and early '60's.

Liddy first drew attention to himself in 1966 while working as an assistant district attorney in Poughkeepsie, New York. Timothy Leary, an occasional lecturer at Harvard University and one of the most durable of headline catchers, was arrested on a drug charge in that Hudson Valley community. Liddy, although only peripherally involved, took public credit.

Determined to make his way in politics, he parlayed the Leary case into the qualifications for a primary race against Hamilton Fish, Republican incumbent of the Twenty-eighth Congressional District. Liddy toured the district stressing the law-and-order theme. In the midst of each public appearance, he would remove his jacket and reveal his shoulder holster. One of his ads during the campaign read, "He knows the answer is law and order, not weak-kneed sociology. Gordon Liddy doesn't bail them out—he puts them in."

Although he lost the Republican nomination to Fish, he was designated by the Conservatives. In that role he could have been a threat to Fish, since the Republican nominee would normally have expected many of his votes to come from Conservative enrollees.

For some reason which he has never explained, ambitious Liddy decided not to campaign as a Conservative, and instead publicly supported Fish.

In April, 1969, Congressman Fish recommended Liddy for a job as special assistant to Assistant Secretary of the Treasury, Eugene T. Rossides. Liddy, a gun buff since his days in the FBI, was assigned duties in the area of fire arms control and narcotics. However, his irrepressible nature would not allow him to settle into a bureaucratic rut. He is remembered by his colleagues as "a staff man who kept trying to set policy."

Liddy's fascination with guns led him to make an unauthorized speech to the National Rifle Association in April, 1971. In it he injudiciously spoke out against gun controls. Within a few months he was discharged by the Treasury Department, according to one official, "because we couldn't control him."

Within days, Egil ("Bud") Krogh, Jr., thirty-one, had recommended Liddy for the spy apparatus in the White House. Krogh had a reputation for efficiency and a tough-minded approach to his work. Dr. Daniel X. Freedman, chairman of the Psychiatry Department of the University of Chicago, a well-known authority on the effect of drugs on mental states, described a meeting with Krogh in which the young government official's grim determination to have his way showed through.

Krogh had asked Dr. Freedman to support legislation which would create a permanent White House office to deal with narcotics traffic and drug abuse. Dr. Freedman refused to support such legislation. Krogh's grim response was, "Well, don't worry. Anyone who opposes us we'll destroy. As a matter of fact, anyone who doesn't support us we'll destroy."

Dr. Freedman told the Associated Press on May 9, 1973, "I do think the language was excessive. I remember thinking at the time that Krogh was referring to destruction of people in Congress who opposed the President rather than to destruction of me, but I was very uneasy about the thing for several years."

Krogh was an assistant to John Ehrlichman, chief adviser to the President on domestic matters and head of the White House Domestic Council, the siamese twin of the Foreign Policy Council run by Henry Kissinger. Thus, youthful Krogh was only one intermediary away from the President. He served on Ehrlichman's Domestic Council as advisor on criminal justice.

In the summer of 1971, as the leaks of information were increasingly peturbing the President, Krogh and Ehrlichman were called into his presence. He complained bitterly about an August 12 story regarding a Soviet move to avert a war by entering a pact with India. In an affidavit he filed with the Los Angeles federal court, Krogh said he "was personally instructed by President Nixon . . . to move ahead with the greatest urgency to determine the source of the 'leaks' " of information on the SALT talks.

Charged with this Presidential responsibility, and urged on by Ehrlichman, Krogh apparently felt grateful that a man with Liddy's qualifications and élan was available. Both Liddy and Hunt had been on Ehrlichman's payroll for over 9 months; Liddy, full-time, Hunt on $100 per diem.

Hunt, a CIA agent for twenty years, now retired, was the writer of many detective novels, among which were *I Came To Kill, House Dick* and *End of a Stripper*. He was given quarters with Liddy in what became known by the conspirators as "Room 16." Hunt's title was White House "consultant."

The fourth member of this spy nucleus was David Young, Krogh's White House assistant. Room 16 was set up in mid-July in the Executive Office Building, under his direct supervision. Hunt was also given an office on the third floor of the White House.

The first duties of the group were to do research and coordinate assignments that had to be made in order to trace the leaks. In the White House they were referred to as "the Plumbers." It was going to be their responsibility to find out what the FBI had been unable to discover for the previous two years.

They were, in effect, an extra-legal police force, beholden only to the President, bound by no laws. They were in the White House to provide services no honest cop would render, and were there covertly at the behest of the President of the United States.

They immediately set up the taps Mitchell had been unwilling to ask Hoover to provide. In addition, there were daily FBI reports on Pentagon Paper developments made available to them, and weekly summaries, elaborately indexed. In the reports was the tantalizing fact that Ellsberg had been under psychiatric care.

Krogh decided that it would be expeditious to get a look at Ellsberg's psychiatric file, in this way obtaining an instant read-out on his personality. The government had indicted Ellsberg for the first time, and Krogh thought such information might be just what was needed to destroy him.

According to Hunt the idea of breaking into the office of Ellsberg's psychiatrist, Dr. Lewis J. Fielding, "became a topic of low-key conversation around the office." When the facts began to come out, John Ehrlichman admitted that he'd wanted the information, but originally claimed to have known nothing about this "office talk."

Hunt innocently asked Krogh, Young, and Liddy, "Well, if you want the materials, why can't we just simply get the FBI to prepare it?"

The answer was that the FBI had stopped handling such matters in the "last five or six years." To a similar question about the Secret Service, he was told, "the White House did not have sufficient confidence in the

Secret Service in order to entrust them with a task of this sort."

The Secret Service was apparently too honest for this sort of work. There was no way out: if a break-in was going to be committed, they would have to be the burglars.

Liddy and Hunt were authorized by Krogh and Young, passing on orders from above, to fly out to Los Angeles to make "a preliminary *vulnerability and feasibility study.*" In short, the break-in was authorized. It was simply a matter of finding out whether it could be done.

Colson, who was special counsel to the President, kept close tabs on the operation. He was in charge of approving vouchers for Hunt's $100 a day stipend. He admitted knowing that the "Plumbers" (Krogh, Young, Hunt, and Liddy) "were going to the West Coast," but he did not know which of them were making the trip, or exactly what their purpose was.

In preparation for the trip, it was decided, special equipment would be needed for the two prospective burglers. Since the CIA specialized in clandestine operations, the decision was to go to them for the provisions.

There was something so hairbrained about this decision that for weeks after the CIA's involvement with the break-in became known, it was assumed that youthful Krogh or Young had "in their zeal" amateurously overstepped themselves.

The CIA was America's answer to foreign espionage efforts after World War II. So antithetical was its existence to American traditions that the men in charge of it, most notably Allen Dulles, its organizer, had scrupulously maintained his Congressional commitment not to take part in any domestic spying activity. Dulles was aware that if knowledge of any such activity reached Congress, the very existence of the organization would be threatened.

However, on July 22, 1971, with his path cleared by a telephone call, E. Howard Hunt made his way to the Langley, Virginia, office of CIA deputy director

General Robert Cushman and, after presenting his White House identification pass, said he "had been authorized to conduct a very sensitive operation by the White House and . . . it should be held a very secret matter."

He told the general that he was required to elicit information and that, in order to accomplish this, he would like "some flash alias documentation and physical disguise."

Cushman, tranquilized by the call he had previously received from the White House, directed a CIA technician to meet Hunt the next day in an agency "safehouse." This was a building where people on CIA business could meet and transact business without fear of being interrupted, identified or overheard.

At this time, and at a subsequent safehouse rendezvous, Hunt and Liddy were outfitted with forged Social Security cards, Hertz Credit Cards, Florida drivers licenses, a 1961 Racket Club membership card, plastic devices to slip under their palates so as to alter their voices, a black wig, a tape recorder, film, and a camera which fit into a tobacco pouch.

In retrospect, none of the elaborate cloak-and-dagger devices were needed. Liddy and Hunt were not planning to break into Dr. Fielding's office themselves. All they were doing was involving the CIA in a domestic crime.

On August 25, Hunt and Liddy flew out to Los Angeles and reconnoitered Dr. Fielding's office. One conspirator took pictures of the other posing in front of the building so that their photographic efforts would appear natural.

The next day, using "a sterile number" provided by the CIA technician—an unlisted number for which no billing was made out—Hunt telephoned his contact and asked to be met at Dulles Airport outside Washington. At that time he handed him the film, which was later returned to him. The subjects on the film appeared so innocent that it would have been perfectly safe to be developed by Kodak.

The next day General Cushman ordered Hunt cut off from any other access to agency help, since his suspicions had been aroused—perhaps from the film—that he was involved in "domestic clandestine operations."

Hunt later drew up an affidavit in which he told of writing out "a series of paragraphs that described the operation . . . the photos were . . . attached, and then the decision was awaited."

After more than a week, word came through that everything was A-OK for the mission.

Hunt was asked, as he put it, "whether or not as a result of my old CIA contacts, I could come up with a team capable to make such an entry."

Hunt flew down to Miami and contacted Bernard L. Barker, a real estate operator in the growing Cuban community who had a strong anti-Castro reputation and who had taken part in the Bay of Pigs attempt to overthrow the Cuban government.

"Mr. Barker," Hunt confessed, "said that he would be very glad to help in a national security operation, which is how I described the operation to him."

Barker then enlisted Felipe de Diego and Eugenio R. Martinez, two Cuban refugees with a generally similar background to his own. Demonstrating his trust in Barker, Hunt merely asked to have them "run past me." In this informal manner, three of the foot-soldiers in the Watergate break-in were placed on the payroll.

Hunt was strong on written material. Part of the reason he had been hired by Ehrlichman was that he was a competent researcher and writer. Not knowing who might be interested in his activities, Hunt acted according to his nature.

"I incorporated my observations of the Cuban part of the entry team in a *memorandum* so that the whole proposition was available *for whoever was going to make the final decision*." [Italics added]

The word was not long in coming, and Hunt then sent marching orders to Barker. On September 2, 1971, he purchased three airline tickets under fictitious names and flew with his confederates to Los Angeles, where they joined Hunt and Liddy at the Beverly Hilton Hotel.

The next morning, according to a deposition Felipe

de Diego made to the Dade County, Florida, State Attorney, he, Barker, and Martinez made a visual reconnaissance of the building in which Dr. Fielding had his office. They returned to their hotel room and Barker departed, soon to return with a suitcase containing photographic equipment, a spotlight, a 35-mm camera, and other burglary devices.

At 9 P.M. the Cubans entered the building, dressed in delivery men's outfits and carrying the suitcase pasted up with Air Express invoices for Dr. Fielding and stickers reading "Rush Immediately." A Mexican cleaning woman was approached and spoken to in Spanish. She was persuaded to let them place the suitcase containing the photographic equipment in Dr. Fielding's office. As they were departing, they punched the unlock button on the outside door leading to the street.

At 1 A.M., September 3, they returned. Finding the door locked, they went around to the rear. While Liddy maintained contact with the three Cubans by walkie-talkie from a cruising car and Hunt watched Dr. Fielding's home, the burglers used masking tape and a glass cutter to break a window in a ground floor office. Having gained entrance to the building, they made their way to the second floor office of Dr. Fielding, where they jimmied the door.

Barker, the leader of the Cubans, now told his two companions, "We are looking for a file of Dr. Daniel Ellsberg." The files were forced open. Felipe de Diego claims they quickly found what they were looking for and he helped hold papers from what appeared to be Dr. Ellsberg's file while Martinez photographed them.

Hunt maintained, "It was reported to me that they had gone through every file in Dr. Fielding's office, including the one in his desk, and that there had been absolutely no material in it with the name of Ellsberg on it."

Back in the Beverly Hilton Hotel they discussed the job, and Liddy and Hunt advised the Miami mafiosa to catch the next plane and get out of town.

Hunt, apparently convinced he should be paid for his efforts, turned in a voucher, subsequently signed by Colson. White House time-and-pay records show he claimed to have worked four hours on September 2, four hours on the day of the break-in (no record of a request for night differential), and two hours for September 4, the day he flew back to Washington. The American Airlines stewardess on that flight told government attorneys that Hunt had struck up a conversation with her and later sent her a book as a gift. The gift was accompanied with a letter on White House stationery signed "Hamilton," the alias used by Hunt on the break-in expedition. Colson also approved a $2,000 expense account for the cost of the flights.

Back in Washington, Hunt claims to have informed Krogh that "it was a clean operation—there were no fingerprints left behind—but it had failed to produce." The Plumbers thought of returning to California for a search of Fielding's home, but although not deterred by the thought that such an act was a serious crime, they decided to abort the idea because it was "too risky."

Hunt now tried to see his friend Colson and tell him what had happened. Colson reports finding him in his outer office. Hunt maintains he informed Colson he was on his way to give a briefing on what "they" had learned about Ellsberg, but since he had about a half hour before the briefing, "he wanted to talk to Colson about it."

Obviously Hunt would not talk to anyone unfamiliar with his activity. However, Colson says he told Hunt he "did not have time to talk to him then—that he was in a hurry." Hunt, apparently a sensitive man, remembers his old friend as being rather brusque. "I don't want to hear anything about it," he quotes him as saying before rushing off.

One can understand Colson's unwillingness to support Hunt's version of his bad manners. If Hunt is to be believed, it indicates Colson knew about "it" in September, 1971. And since "it" was a crime, it meant he had failed to report to the police an event which he, as a lawyer, knew he must report. So it is much safer to claim having rushed off and to insist, "Hunt did not try to broach the subject matter again."

The attempts to plead ignorance of the crime eventually came from all quarters of the compass. The Los Angeles police, anxious to tidy up the docket, arrested a suspect on October 7, one month later. He was E. Davis, 43, who had been arrested ninety times since 1942. He had been picked up for the alleged theft of a woman's purse.

The police showed him a copy of the report of the burglary of Dr. Fielding's office, and another report of the break-in at a doctor's office on the first floor, which they mistakenly carried as a separate crime. Davis complained on November 12, 1971, that a police officer had told him that if he would help him "clean up the books on several crimes," he would intercede with the district attorney's office on his behalf. Although the police records show Davis confessed to burglarizing Dr. Fielding's office in search of narcotics, he was never prosecuted, and instead was punished for parole violation because of the purse theft.

Back in 1971, no one suspected the true nature of the crime. It was not even necessary for the men involved in its planning and execution to invent plausible alibis. Is it any wonder that they became bolder?

When the prosecutors at Daniel Ellsberg's expensive mistrial finally felt constrained to turn over the information they had on the White House break-in at the office of Ellsberg's psychiatrist, cover stories were a dime a dozen.

Most twisted of all was the story told by John Ehrlichman. This was the same Ehrlichman who had been put in charge of the Plumbers when Nixon had insisted some way must be found to shut off the leaks.

He informed the FBI interrogators on April 27, 1973, that "sometime in 1971 the President had . . . asked him to make inquiries independent of concurrent FBI investigation" about Pentagon Paper leaks. He knew

Liddy and Hunt were "designated to conduct this investigation."

Then, in an attempt to prove how candid he was being, he admitted knowing "Liddy and Hunt conducted investigations in the Washington, D.C., area and during the inquiries were going to the West Coast to follow up on leads."

However, although he knew they were going to California, he "was not told that these two individuals had broken into the premises of the psychiatrist for Ellsberg until after this incident had taken place."

Furthermore, the FBI affidavit recorded, "Such activity was not authorized by him, he did not know about this burglary until after it had happened. He did 'not agree with this method of investigation' and when he learned about the burglary he instructed them 'not to do this again.'"

He concluded by assuring the FBI agents, "He does not know whose idea it was to commit this burglary" and "has no knowledge whether anything was obtained as a result of this activity."

On May 10, soon after Mr. Ehrlichman's new position was explosively revealed in the press, Mr. Colson was brought before the grand jury. It was preparing to hand up indictments on some of his closest friends. Oh, yes, he now recalled, he had known of the burglary, although he had not heard about it from Hunt. He had been at a meeting with Mr. Ehrlichman, at which time the President's lieutenant told him of the second-story job done on Dr. Fielding's office.

Both Ehrlichman and Colson, two men on whose honor the day-to-day functioning of the American government depended, had suddenly confessed knowledge of a burglary. Although they were both lawyers and knew of their responsibility to report the crime to the police, neither of them had done so. In fact, they had made every effort to conceal their knowledge of the crime.

Colson apparently felt that since he had been informed of the felony by his boss, it was not his responsibility to override his superior's judgment. Ehrlichman, on the other hand, seemed to feel that having told the burglars "not to do this again," they had been sufficiently punished, so that further penalties from a criminal court were not necessary.

The arrogance involved in this decision is apparent immediately. What was not as apparent was the duplicity still being practiced by Ehrlichman and the men around the President even at this late date.

On May 11, 1973, the day after Colson's testimony before the grand jury, Marine Corps Commandant General Robert Cushman was called before three Congressional Committees and shocked the nation with revelations about his role in the burglary.

Cushman had been Richard Nixon's military advisor during the 1950's. As his leader rose through the ranks, Cushman followed. In 1971, while the Plumbers and their foreman were concocting their scheme, Cushman had made his way as far as Deputy Director of the CIA.

Cushman testified before the House Armed Services Subcommittee, then marched across the floor of the Capital Building and told essentially the same story to the Senate Appropriations Subcommittee, and finally read off his three-page statement to the Senate Armed Services Committee. All of these committees were investigating the possibility the CIA, which is excluded by its charter from taking part in internal security matters, had seriously overstepped its authority.

Decked out in full uniform, stars glittering from his shoulders, his chest decked with rows of battle ribbons, a sharpshooter's medal hanging from the bottom row, Cushman had been called back from Europe the previous day. He marched from one committee to another, grim visaged, refusing to even acknowledge the shouted questions of reporters.

His story was as simple as it was shocking. On July 3, 1971, he had received a telephone call from John Ehrlichman. He had known Ehrlichman "for ten to twelve years," and respected him highly. Ehrlichman called from the White House. "He identified Hunt as a bona fide employee of the White House." He then told Cushman that Hunt was a consultant on security matters. In that capacity Hunt was going to need the agency's assistance from time to time. He asked Cushman to make sure such assistance was provided.

Cushman testified, "I also knew that he [Ehrlichman] was one of the three chiefs of staff, as it were, to the President, and that therefore he spoke with the authority of the President's name."

As far as he was concerned, he told the Senators, "I felt the request came in from the boss."

Fifteen days later, on July 22, Hunt had put in his appearance in Cushman's office. He told the general he had "a very sensitive one-time interview that the White House wanted him to hold," and he needed CIA paraphernalia. Hunt referred to Ehrlichman by name and Cushman acknowledged he had earlier received a call from Ehrlichman.

Determined to cooperate with Ehrlichman's request, Cushman issued the necessary authorization. A few days later, he said, he went to the director of the CIA, Richard M. Helms, and told him of Ehrlichman's call and Hunt's visit. According to Cushman, Helms "assented to what I had done."

It appears from testimony given by the man who had succeeded Helms as director of the international spy agency, James L. Schlesinger, that Helms had already compromised the CIA. He told a Senate investigating subcommittee on May 9, 1973, that Helms had personally instructed officers of the agency to assist in preparing a "psychiatric profile" on Ellsberg. The CIA had done many such profiles on officials of foreign governments. But this was the first time in its existence it had worked up a domestic profile. In doing so it was violating its charter. Schlesinger described the CIA's role in the Ellsberg affair as "ill-advised." Apparently Helms, having violated this CIA canon at least once, found an additional infraction of the law not worth a second thought.

Despite Helms' endorsement, Cushman felt uneasy. As the weeks passed he found Hunt "was becoming more and more unreasonable and demanding," and was seeking more aid than he considered necessary for "a one-time interview."

As a result, the general decided to stop "all relationships" with Hunt. This was approximately one day after the first reconnoiter trip to Los Angeles, and more than a week before the burglary. As soon as he had made up his mind, he got on the phone with Ehrlichman and informed him of his decision. Then, he testified, he told Ehrlichman in no uncertain terms that "in my opinion, Mr. Hunt was of questionable judgment."

Despite Cushman's well-intentioned warning, Ehrlichman continued—and intensified—his use of Hunt and Liddy. This did not keep him from hiding the fact. Almost a year and a half later, Ehrlichman was still trying to obfuscate any attempt to link him to the White House espionage apparatus. On December 12, 1972, Ronald Zeigler, his integrity still not effectively destroyed, addressed a news conference. He responded to questions by admitting Egil Krogh and David Young had been assigned to investigate a "series of news reports relating to a great extent to national security affairs." Yes, as part of that effort they had been provided with a private phone, one not connected through the White House switchboard.

In response to further questions from reporters, who at this stage of the Watergate investigations were beginning to suspect the case might be about to burst open, Zeigler said it was his understanding that E. Howard Hunt and G. Gordon Liddy had not been involved in the project, and that Bernard Barker had not been called on the private telephone.

Zeigler warned that "to attempt to associate this with anything that happened after January of 1972 [the planning sessions for the Watergate break-in], in fact, through suggestion or through association with individuals who fell into bad times later in the year of 1972, would be folly on the part of those who attempted to do that."

Then in an effort to defend John Ehrlichman from even the suggestion of improper conduct, Zeigler said Ehrlichman had been unaware the bills for the private telephone were paid by his office.

It was clear that Ehrlichman, despite his and Zeigler's protestations, had known a great deal about the activities of Hunt and Liddy. He was so sure of Hunt's needs in the summer of 1971 that he had phoned a top espionage official, General Cushman, on whose loyalty he felt he could depend, and asked him to supply the soon-to-be burglar with his tools. That he knew there was a sinister purpose to Hunt's mission can be reasonably assumed, even without his subsequent confession that he knew Dr. Fielding's office had been burglarized and had done nothing about it. Had Hunt's mission been innocent, there would have been no need to seek the aid of undercover agents.

The facts surrounding the burglary of Dr. Fielding's office did not begin to emerge for more than ten months after the Watergate break-in. By the time it did, Watergate had become a *cause célèbre,* unmatched, in its way, in American history.

The burglary, done with direction from many of the same men later involved in Watergate, added a sinister dimension to that *cause célèbre.* Men sitting in the White House, daily offering advice to the President, had planned and supervised a felony. They had been illegally tapping phones for years. They had involved the CIA in a domestic crime. And then, in a manner most cold, they had obstructed the federal prosecutor's attempt to obtain justice by perjuring themselves.

If the President were to speak of the Fielding burglary, as he did of the Watergate break-in, he would undoubtedly say he did not know about the plot. There is, however, ample evidence the President played an active role in trying to suppress the facts in Ellsberg's case.

The key affidavits which support this statement resulted from action taken by White House chief counsel John Wesley Dean III on April 15, 1973. Dean was earlier in bad odor with the Nixon junta after proclaiming he was not going to be made a "scapegoat" in the Watergate fiasco. In an effort to gain immunity from prosecution in return for supplying evidence, Dean went to Watergate chief prosecutor Earl J. Silbert on that fateful April 15. Dean revealed for the first time that Hunt and Liddy, acting under White House orders, had burglarized Dr. Fielding's office.

Silbert wrote out a memo on Dean's allegations and turned it over to Assistant Attorney General Henry E. Petersen, who had recently been given complete charge of the Watergate investigation. Petersen recognized the incendiary nature of the memo and took it directly to the President. The next day, April 17, Nixon threw his bombshell.

Before a hastily assembled news conference, reading a vague statement about "major" new findings which he expected to result in indictments, Nixon gave his answer to Dean. The wording was so Aesopian that only Dean and those involved in the intrigue of the previous two days understood the full meaning of what he was saying.

"I have expressed to the appropriate authorities," he said with a sudden note of firmness, "my view that no individual holding, in the past or at present, a position of major importance in the Administration should be given immunity from prosecution."

The first reaction was that the President had, with that righteous pronouncement, heralded a new policy of cooperation with those attempting to run down the truth. However, legal voices were quickly heard to point out that he had actually moved to silence potential high-ranking turncoats. Dean did not need their explanation to make absolutely clear to him what he had heard.

But the day before Nixon's bombshell, Assistant Attorney General Petersen informed the President that it was going to be necessary to forward Dean's statement to Judge Byrne, since the prosecution of Ellsberg now appeared to be based on information obtained illegally. He pointed out that, under the so-called Brady rule, it was necessary for the prosecution to report all information to the defense in a criminal trial which might help to clear the accused.

Richard Nixon's reaction: Petersen was ordered not to release the information about Liddy and Hunt's crime. His explanation: the release of the information might adversely affect "national security."

The *Times* and *Washington Post* both reported that Petersen was shaken by Nixon's stand. According to the *Post,* he "didn't know what to do he was so upset. He had to get this straightened out so he could live with his own children." The *Times* said, "He just couldn't live with himself."

After two days of torment, Petersen went to Richard Kleindienst, then serving out his last days as Attorney General. They debated the matter for hours, and then Kleindienst decided to see the President. Nixon listened to Kleindienst's practical advice and agreed to have the news of the break-in forwarded to Los Angeles.

Judge Byrne received the content of Silbert's memo on April 26. He then proceeded to make life difficult for those trying to suppress knowledge of the crime. He released the news of the burglary, and compounded his action by ordering a government investigation of the episode. That same day, Friday, April 27, FBI agents visited in the White House with Haldeman and Ehrlichman.

At this point the cover on the Fielding burglary was being lifted. Ehrlichman made out his affidavit implicating Krogh. When Krogh heard about it, he determined to break his silence. First he spoke to Ehrlichman. The President's confidant attempted to persuade him not to disclose what he knew about the details of the burglary. Krogh quoted him as saying repeatedly and emphatically, "The President doesn't want any more of this to surface for national security reasons." Ehrlichman characterized the President's action as being "an attempt to keep the lid on."

Krogh, no longer as sure of himself as he had been when the light of Presidential approval had shone on his efforts, spent several days trying to make up his mind what to do. Was he, in effect, to go against the leader of his country? Was he to betray the confidence of the men who had been responsible for him, at such a relatively young age, advancing so far?

He decided to discuss his dilemma with Elliott Richardson, by then designated to replace the resigned Kleindienst as Attorney General. Richardson was the Secretary of Defense and had the reputation of being a clever lawyer and a man of integrity. They had lunch together. Krogh told Richardson about the initial operation and about the President's insistence that further details not be revealed. Richardson was "horrified." He told Krogh he completely disagreed with the President's position that "national security" was involved in the Liddy-Hunt burglary.

Richardson is reputed to have remarked, "I'm not going to participate in a cover-up because it will destroy my role in the Watergate investigation. I'm not going to follow through on the President's orders."

Krogh's resolve was strengthened by his talk with Richardson, and he drafted the affidavit which was sent to Judge Byrne on May 7 and immediately released to the press.

Among the startling things Krogh swore to was that he was "informed by the Federal Bureau of Investigation that the so-called Pentagon papers were in the possession of the Soviet Embassy, Washington, D. C., prior to their publication by the *New York Times*."

If this was true, it meant that when Ellsberg gave his copy to the *Times* the Nixon Administration knew it was no longer an absolute secret. The contents of the Papers had always been described by scholars and newspapermen as being information widely known to them. But this was the first allegation that, despite their staleness, the Soviet embassy was known to have their content long before the *Times* subscribers.

Most damning of all was Krogh's claim that after the

CIA psychological profile of Ellsberg had "provided no useful information . . . general authorization to engage in covert activity to obtain a psychological history [of Ellsberg] or ascertain associates of Dr. Fielding was thereafter given to the special unit *by John D. Ehrlichman*." [Italics added]

Krogh was publicly, and under oath, declaring that Ehrlichman had directly authorized a secret effort to obtain information not available legally.

It had become clear that, long before Watergate, there were substantial grounds for the impeachment of several "civil officers" at the very top of the Nixon Administration.

# CHAPTER IX

## *Again National Security*

The failure of the Fielding burglary to produce results to which the felons could point with pride did not diminish their supervisors' faith in their ability. As in the case of many bureaucratic schemes, once set in motion the results of a great effort were not as important as the fact the effort was being made vigorously.

So it was that, blessed with an expensive failure, which had been made suitably impressive with CIA contrivances, code names, flights to far corners of the country, vouchers, and a requisite number of memoranda, a new assignment was found for Ehrlichman's underlings.

The matter began innocently enough. Charles Colson informed Hunt that he was being assigned to a "research" project. Since it was possible Edward Kennedy might be Richard Nixon's opponent in the 1972 election, a dossier must be started on him.

This time there was no justification for Hunt's assignment on the basis of national security. There was no thought that Kennedy was involved in the publication of the Pentagon Papers, or that he was leaking administration secrets to the press. It was simply a matter of finding out if there was any undiscovered dirt which might be useful when the mudslinging season began the following year.

Hunt, decked out with an alias, went up to Chappaquiddick to see if anyone might be found who could supply some wretched item which would further discredit the Massachusetts Senator. The death of Kennedy's secretary in an automobile accident had already been used in an attempt at political sabotage. In August, 1971, a Harris poll about Chappaquiddick had been reprinted on stationery bearing an Edmund Muskie letterhead. It was bogus, but was clever enough to cut up two Democrats. It reminded everyone of the Kennedy failure that terrible night, and made Muskie look like a cad willing to backstab a colleague in order to advance his ambitions.

Colson's fertile mind was employed in thinking of ideas which might aid in the President's reelection. After Colson's peccadilloes started to come to light, Lyn Nofziger, an official of the Republican National Committee, revealed that he had rejected a number of Colson campaign ideas. They ranged, he said, from "dangerous" to "idiotic."

One of his choicer plots again employed Hunt's conspiratorial talents. He ordered the espionage story writer to research the death of South Vietnam's President Ngo Dinh Diem. A rumor had been floating around for years that John F. Kennedy had ordered Diem's death at the time of the military coup which overthrew his corrupt government. It had been fairly well established that Diem had been overthrown with State Department blessings. Cables quoted in the Pentagon Papers supported that contention. However, such Machiavellian orders to cut Diem down were to this moment only the speculation of those who wanted to think the worst of the assassinated President. Colson now directed Hunt to find the proof.

David Young, who had been working for Henry Kissinger until July, 1971, when he was transferred to Ehrlichman's staff, was assigned to clear the way for Hunt's scholarship. He phoned the office of Under Secretary of State William B. Macomber, Jr., on September 20, 1971, and asked that Hunt be given access to Saigon cable traffic from April 1 through November 30, 1963.

Many of the documents in question were classified *secret* and required a security clearance for those wishing to inspect them. No such clearance was demanded of Hunt. After this call from out of the blue, it was only necessary for him to walk into the State Department and show a White House pass to be given all the privileges normally reserved for those on legitimate business.

Underscoring the laxness of the procedures was the State Department spokesman's remark that Hunt "would not divulge his purpose in inspecting the cable traffic to those who were assisting him in our records service division."

Finally, this unknown person, on an unknown mission, was permitted to "take with him copies of some two hundred and forty cables." Hunt took the papers back to Room 16 and began a careful study of them. He compared them to the Ellsberg version of the Pentagon Papers and thought he detected that a number of the cables were missing. Hunt remarked in his testimony to the grand jury, released May 7, 1973, that "there came a time when I mentioned this to Mr. Colson, who had been directing my research . . ."

The sworn testimony before the grand jury speaks eloquently of the relationship of these two men. After explaining his doubts to Colson, Hunt told the jury:

"And he said, 'Well, what kind of material have you dug up on the files that would indicate Kennedy complicity?'

"And I showed him three or four cables that indicated that they had pretty close to pull[ed] the trigger against Premier Diem's head, but it didn't say so in so many words. Inferentially, one could say that it was a high degree of administration complicity in the actual assassination of Diem and his brother.

"And he said, 'Well, this isn't good enough. Do you think you could improve on them?'

"I said, 'Yes, I probably could, but not without technical assistance.'

"So he said, 'Well, we won't be able to give you any technical help. This is too hot. See what you can do on your own.' "

If Hunt is to be believed, then Colson—with full understanding of the nature of what he was saying—was ordering his willing subordinate to forge the missing documents. Hunt's testimony to the grand jury indicated that once he heard the order, he set about his task with relish.

"So, with the very meager means at my disposal, which were literally a Xerox machine in the White House, a razor blade and a typewriter—which was not the same one as had been used on the original cables— I set about creating two cables . . ."

A professional pride, not repressed by the months Hunt had already spent in jail before he spoke to the grand jury, breaks through his unembarrassed description of the crime.

"The process was relatively simple. I first of all prepared a cable text. In other words, from many of these cables I could pretty well adjust the text to the type of language that would be used by the man who was the ostensible originator, and altered these, from time to time, until I was satisfied that I had two creditable cables.

"I was not satisfied with the result. I showed them to Colson. He seemed to like them and I said, 'These will never stand any kind of scrutiny.' "

Urged on by Colson, Hunt tried to improve his forgery. He confessed that he "asked the FBI to tell me what kind of type face had been used on the original State Department cables." In this moment of excess, thoughtless enthusiasm, he was involving Hoover's agency in a crime. Having shown them a State Department cable he intended to use in creating a forgery, his main regret was that "I found out that it would be impossible for me to get access to a similar type-face."

Finally conceding he had run up against a stone wall, he concluded, almost petulantly:

"So I knew this was a technical problem that could not be overcome. So if anybody was going to see these cables, they'd simply have to see them. They could never be published, because after the Alger Hiss case, everyone was typewriter conscious.

"So there would just have to be a fast brush show on

a take-it-or-leave-it basis, which I began to believe was the purpose Mr. Colson had in mind."

In the midst of his testimony, Hunt gave an insight into the life he had been leading prior to his employment by the Nixon Administration. With a note of pride, he explained why he thought he might succeed in forging the cables. "After all, I had been given some training in my past CIA career to do just this sort of thing and had done it successfully on numerous occasions, floating forged newspaper accounts, telegrams, that sort of thing."

Did he mention this when Ehrlichman interviewed him for the job?

Hunt's cable, dated October 23, 1963, three days before the assassination of Diem and his brother, was labeled an "instruction" to Henry Cabot Lodge. After its final polishing, it read:

"At highest level meeting [Washingtonian code language for *a meeting with the President*] today, decision reluctantly made that . . . . granting asylum or otherwise protecting the brothers certain to alienate if not enrage generals. . . . Moreover, leaders of successful coup deserve clean slate in SVN [South Vietnam], which they likely achieve by making sure neither brother survives."

Apparently satisfied with what Hunt showed him, Colson looked around for someone past whom he could "brush" the forgery. He settled on William G. Lambert, then working out his last few months as a reporter for the soon defunct *Life* Magazine.

Colson, in the manner of a high administration official about to leak a story, advised Lambert to reread President Nixon's press conference remarks of September 16, 1971.

At that time the President had stated, "I would remind all concerned that the way we got into Vietnam was through overthrowing Diem and the complicity in the murder of Diem . . ."

This was a simplistic, in fact, inaccurate way of describing our entry in that longest of American wars. Years before Diem's assassination on November 1, 1963, the United States was deeply involved in the war. President Eisenhower had sent "advisors" and "technicians" to Vietnam as far back as 1954. In view of Nixon's well-documented efforts to involve American soldiers in the fighting, and his vigorous endorsement of President Kennedy's Vietnam policy in 1963, his press conference remarks seem to do the dead President an injustice.

Having done his homework, Lambert returned to Colson. The Presidential counsel then referred him to Hunt, informing him that Hunt had an explosive disclosure to make about the murder of Diem. Toward the end of 1971 or the beginning of 1972, Lambert later revealed, Hunt showed him "about fifty" protocopies of what appeared to be diplomatic messages relating to the last months of Diem's life. He would not give him copies of the messages, but allowed him to write them out in his own hand.

The two forgeries had melodramatically been inscribed, "Ambassador Lodge—Eyes Only." It appeared to be signed by six government officials, including McGeorge Bundy, then special assistant to President Kennedy. As though to guarantee its authenticity, it had stamped on it the name "Rusk."

Lambert spent months trying to verify the cables. *Life* editors finally decided not to use the story. Lambert maintained his trust in Colson for some time after the Watergate disclosures, and even after Colson left the White House in March, 1973, to go into private law practice.

However, he finally brought himself to question Colson at his Virginia home at the end of April. At first Colson denied knowing the cables were fraudulent. A week later he told a persistent Lambert he had indeed known the documents were forgeries as far back as February, 1972. He still denied he "ordered" Hunt to forge the documents, but he no longer denied he had seen the phony cables, or that he had supervised Hunt's attempts to establish President Kennedy's complicity in Diem's murder.

On Saturday, April 28, 1973, reporters attempted to find out whether President Nixon's September 16, 1971, press conference statement implicating President Kennedy in Diem's assassination was based on the forged cables. Nixon was in retreat at the mountaintop Camp David, gazing at the distant lights of Washington and pondering what he should do about the mounting crisis in confidence about his administration.

After a suitable pause, the word came back through a spokesman: "The answer is no."

There could be no other answer. For at the time the President struck his blow at John Kennedy, the cables had not yet been forged. It appears possible that one of the main reasons for the forgery, especially in view of Colson's deliberate invitation for Lambert to reread Nixon's remarks before seeing Hunt, was to provide support for a Presidential press conference exaggeration, which had been made intemperately, without any evidence on which it could be based.

Lambert's copy of the forgery remains, but the originals have disappeared. Their disappearance was the occasion for another major crime committed by the Nixon Administration.

Hunt had placed the forged cables in his office safe in the basement of the Executive Office Building. The safe contained other samples of his trade which he did not want laying around on his desk. It included a pistol, electronic bugging equipment, and a psychiatric profile on Ellsberg.

Two and a half days after the June 17, 1972, break-in at Watergate, the contents of Hunt's safe were brought to John Dean's White House office. Dean claimed to have been shocked by what he found and reported immediately to Ehrlichman. According to Dean, Ehrlichman suggested he dump the whole mess into the Potomac on his way home to Alexandria that night.

Dean, a bright young lawyer, realized the seriousness of what was being proposed. Destroying evidence of a probable crime was in itself a serious crime. Instead, he somehow convinced Ehrlichman to trust the destiny of these documents to L. Patrick Gray, the President's new acting head of the FBI.

On June 28, eleven days after the break-in, he handed the documents to Gray in two folders. According to Gray's sworn statement to a Senate Committee, Dean said they contained "political dynamite" and "should never see the light of day."

According to Dean and Gray the White House wanted these documents destroyed. But so conditioned were the men near the throne to having other men do their bidding that, instead of merely taking them to the nearest fireplace and incinerating them, they entangled a gaggle of other geese in their plot.

In the process, they compromised the FBI and destroyed Gray's career. He told the Senators pondering whether to approve his nomination that, a few days later, without looking at the documents, he had placed them in an FBI "burn bag," and that they had subsequently been destroyed. On April 27, 1973, a few hours after his testimony had been made public, Gray resigned as acting director of the FBI.

However, days later he revealed his sworn testimony to the Senate had not been completely true. Instead of placing the documents in the burn bag he had actually taken them home to Connecticut. He had kept them for several months, finally, he claimed, burning them "around Christmas" 1972.

What purpose Gray had in mind is a matter of speculation. No doubt he felt uncomfortable at being put into such a compromised position. But as in the case of Colson, who at the very least admitted he knew the Diem cables were forgeries as far back as February, 1972, he concealed his knowledge of a crime. In so doing, he became a participant in the crime.

The clearest pattern that emerges from the early activities of the White House task force in charge of burglary, forgery, sabotage, perjury and other assorted felonies, was their mindless determination to involve the CIA, the FBI, and the State Department, three of the most sensitive and powerful agencies of government, in the most corrupt conspiracies it could invent.

CHAPTER X

## Oh What a Tangled Web
## We Weave . . .

There are those who profess to see a major difference between the crimes associated with the Nixon Administration and those associated with earlier administrations similarly begrimed. The difference, they maintain, is that those earlier crimes were committed for profit, whereas Nixon's men committed theirs out of affection, loyalty, and perhaps an inordinate yearning to wield power.

Although there are undoubtedly elements of truth to this theory, a common motive often seemed to inspire both sets of villains. The crimes committed by Grant and Harding's cronies were transparently for money. It was piled up on their desks in bags of gold and stacks of stock certificates.

The crimes committed by Nixon's men were just as clearly for a profit, although the profit was manifested more subtly. What greater profit could an agency man imagine than to sit at the foot of the throne, beckoning suppliants forth or waving them aside.

Colson saw himself as Governor of California; Ehrlichman was to be Senator from Washington. Who knew where the road led from there?

Clearly the styles were different. The Grant and Harding bunch over-ate. The men around Nixon watched their cholesterol count. The earlier miscreants enjoyed their booze and were never happier than when they were gambling and carousing. Haldeman was a Christian Scientist, along with the men around him, an abstainer, addicted to simple dress and plain talk.

Yet there is something absurd about the idea that

calculating, emotionless men like Haldeman and Ehrlichman would exert themselves for gratitude. More
absurd was the thought that Richard Nixon, the most
private of all public men, could so inspire a comradely
feeling in the breasts of these cynics that they would
perjure and steal in order to give him an extra moment's
comfort.

The greatest profits are often those for which one is
forced to wait. Grab the money and run, which seems
to have been the working slogan of Belknap, Forbes,
and Fall, was the mark of a simpler day. The new men
in the White House had come to power in a more so-
phisticated age.

Nixon had shown the way. A poor man when he entered politics, he was now a millionaire. No doubt they
saw even greater piles of gold further down the road.
There was no need to grab it now, when a flood of it
would pour on them as soon as they entered private life.
And they were such careful men that thoughts of mislaid
plans or spoiled dreams had no place in their thinking.
They were going to run a perfect show and then, later,
they were going to receive a perfect reward.

Haldeman was backstopping his expectations by taking an almost daily homemade film record of Nixon's
administration. As a former toiler in the media industry,
he knew the value of such exclusive footage. It was also
out of character for men such as Haldeman, Chapin,
Zeigler, who had taken dead aim from early adulthood
at the largely monetary rewards of commercial advertising, to suddenly have reverted to self-abnegation.

Money, according to the proverb, is the root of all
evil, and it had a role to play in this evil matter.

One of the more shocking aspects of recent political
campaigns has been the extraordinary amounts of
money raised for the simple act of electing public officials. In this quest the Republicans have always out-
raced the Democrats, usually by a two-to-one margin.
In 1964 the Goldwater campaign coffers were stuffed
with in excess of $24,000,000. Nixon's more successful
campaign in 1968 required a more strenuous effort by

his fund raisers. The reported sum was in excess of $35,000,000. Campaign 1972, if one can accept the January 31, 1973 report of the Finance Committee for the Reelection of the President, cost at least $50,000,000.

Altogether more than $400,000,000 was raised by all parties for elections on all levels of government in 1972. The Nixon reelection treasury was swollen by $7,500,000 contributed by a group of eighteen individuals.

To point out that these contributors were not completely selfless, but were expecting service for their coin, is to miss the more important significance of these figures. It had become extraordinarily expensive for a citizen in one of the most democratic countries in the world to run for public office. In short, large numbers of talented people were being denied the privilege of serving the nation because of their inability to mass huge amounts of money behind their candidacy. When one considers the fact that 75 per cent of the $400,000,000 raised in 1972 came from less than one per cent of the population, the subversive impact of money on our democratic election process becomes apparent.

Extremely scrupulous men are repelled by the demands to which the acceptance of such overly generous contributions opens them. They tend to drop out of politics at an early stage, while the field is left to men with stronger stomachs.

The men around Nixon proved to have constitutions of iron. There is not a single indication on the record that they ever voluntarily brought themselves to reject a proferred sum, simply because the donors impulses were impure.

The importance of money in Nixon's 1972 plans became clear even before the need was apparent for sabotage and burglary experts. In March, 1971, Herbert Kalmbach was put in charge of the early fund raising campaign. He opened an account in the Newport Beach branch of the Bank of America on January 28, 1971, and kept it active until the following January 28.

Contributions to this account were legal—and secret.

The campaign contribution law then in operation was so weak that, for all purposes, those who gave Kalmbach money were assured their largess would go unnoticed.

Kalmbach's account grew to $500,000, $40,000 of which was paid to Donald Segretti, a twenty-six year old lawyer just out of the army, to finance his "dirty tricks" —sabotage efforts against the Democrats. Eventually Segretti had fifty saboteurs working for him. One of his "tricks" led to his indictment in Florida on May 4, 1973. He had mailed a fictitious letter on March 11, 1972, during the Democratic primary, on Senator Muskie's stationery, accusing Senators Humphrey and Jackson of sexual misconduct. "Tricks" of this sort had contributed heavily to the destruction of Muskie, the one Democrat Nixon most feared.

Kalmbach had been a fund raiser for Nixon in the 1968 campaign and through his California law firm— Kalmbach, De Marco, Knapp, Chillingworth—handled all of the President's business affairs.

This association brought Kalmbach to the point where, in 1971, it cost $10,000 merely to consult with him on any matter relating to Washington litigation. So effective was his role as fund raiser that contributions of $20,000 after a single telephone call were not uncommon.

Helping Kalmbach in these early efforts was Murray Chotiner, who became the first White House staff member to resign in March, 1971, and to go to work for Nixon's re-election. Chotiner hung his hat at Reeves & Harrison, at 1701 Pennsylvania Avenue, the building which was soon to house the Committee to Re-elect the President. At this early date, Reeves & Harrison was engaged in raising funds for the Nixon campaign, a not uncommon practice for some law firms.

Chotiner and Kalmbach indicated the nature of their efforts in March, 1971, the first month of the finance committee's existence. Dairy farmers were demanding a raise in the price of milk. (Reeves & Harrison, incidentally, represented several of the largest dairy cooperatives.) Since these prices were controlled by the Department of Agriculture, the dairy farmers' plea was made to then Secretary Clifford M. Hardin. Hardin, soon to be jettisoned for the politically astringent Earl Butz, announced in early March that he was denying the price increase.

Chotiner then swung into action. In a deposition he made out on November 28, 1972, in answer to a suit filed by Ralph Nader, he explained that he had taken the dairy farmers' case to four high-ranking White House aides, among them John Ehrlichman and Charles Colson. "I told the gentlemen," Chotiner responded openly, "that, in my opinion, the dairy farmers constituted a very important segment of the population of the country."

Chotiner's message was heard. On March 23, 1971, the President met with dairy cooperative officials. Within twenty-four hours Hardin's decision was reversed and the price of milk was allowed to rise.

In another deposition taken as a result of the Nader suit, Gary E. Hanman, senior executive vice president of Mid-America Dairymen, Inc., testified that dairymen's commitments to contribute to the Nixon campaign "made the difference" in obtaining the reversal of Hardin's price freeze order.

In the face of this declaration, Chotiner maintained he had "nothing to do with those people making contributions." He did admit, however, that before the March 25 price reversal announcement, he knew of the dairymen's plans to make a substantial contribution to Nixon's campaign.

Furthermore, although he wanted the world to believe he had nothing to do with obtaining contributions from milkmen, he conceded that he had arranged for the contributions to be channeled through one hundred separate "paper" finance committees. One of the tin-box organizations went by the title, *The Committee for Better Government.*

Chotiner responded to a question from Nader's lawyer that he had chided the dairy men months after the price increase because "contributions had not been made I understood were going to be made."

But when he had spoken to Ehrlichman and Colson, he insisted, he had not linked the price increase with prospective dairy contributions.

"So, therefore," Nader's lawyer asked, "political contributions of that sort did not figure in any of the discussions in any way?"

Chotiner, who knew that today's confession is forgotten tomorrow, but perjury lands you in jail, responded, "I won't go that far."

In another deposition, George L. Mehren, general manager of Associated Milk Producers, Inc., said Kalmbach asked "quite unequivocally" for dairy contributions, and then tried to shut off the flow of these contributions when the industry leaders insisted on making them public.

Eventually the milk producers gave at least $417,500 —a drop in the bucket.

Perhaps the most blatant example of the corrupting influence of money in the 1972 Nixon campaign occurred when Robert L. Vesco decided to make a contribution.

Vesco's career took an upsurge in 1965 when, age twenty-nine, he created International Controls, a company he wished to make into a conglomerate. In three years he pyramided sales from $2,000,000 to $67,-000,000.

Vesco gained control of International Overseas Services, a mutual fund complex established by Bernard Cornfeld, at the beginning of 1971. The fight to take over Cornfeld's empire had dominated the newspapers of the world for months. Cornfeld had convinced thousands of middle class Europeans that he could make them millionaires. In the process, he had converted himself from a door-to-door salesman of mutual funds to the owner of a castle in France and a Swiss villa built by Napoleon.

Within a short time of pushing Cornfeld out, Vesco had bled the parent company of $224,000,000, which he concealed in banks and dummy corporations under his control.

In March, 1971, just as Kalmbach was renting office space for himself on the second floor of 1701 Pennsylvania Avenue, the Securities and Exchange Commission began its Vesco investigation, which it described as the largest security fraud case on record.

By mid-1971 Vesco was beginning to feel the pressure from SEC investigators. He sent Harry Sears, former Republican majority leader in the New Jersey senate and a director in one of Vesco's firms, to plead his case with Attorney General Mitchell. Sears was also head of Nixon's Jersey reelection campaign.

Vesco had an affinity for people with political clout. Donald Nixon, the twenty-six year old nephew of the President, was hired during this time as Vesco's administrative assistant.

As the SEC pressure increased, Vesco felt constrained to send Sears back to Mitchell. At this January, 1972, meeting Sears asked the Attorney General to arrange a meeting for him with SEC chairman William Casey. He explained he wanted to discuss the Vesco case. Some might find it strange that the head of a firm being investigated for possible criminal activity would have gone to the top man in the Justice Department in an endeavor to make an appointment with his prosecutors in an independent agency. But this was all in a day's work for John Mitchell, who at that time was also being approached by Harold Geneen of International Telephone and Telegraph for help in an anti-trust action.

Tormented by the slowness of Mitchell's reaction, Vesco took the bull by the horns and on March 8, 1972, went to see Maurice Stans, who had recently taken over from Kalmbach as chairman of the Finance Committee for the Re-election of the President. Stans had been Secretary of Commerce, but President Nixon apparently thought rounding up money for his reelection effort, a service performed for him by Stans in the 1968 campaign, was more important.

Vesco offered to feed the Nixon kitty $500,000 if

only Stans and Mitchell would restrain the SEC investigation. At this point Stans is alleged to have shown the better side of his nature. He requested only $250,000, specifying that it was to be in cash. Stans was the acknowledged expert in campaign contributions, and knew when payment should be on the barrelhead.

This was a period of great stress for Stans. The new Federal Elections Campaign Act took effect on April 7, 1972. After that time it would be necessary to reveal the name of large donors and the amount of their contributions. Stans was, therefore, making a herculean push to get substantial contributions, from those who wished to retain their anonymity, into the hands of his committee before the deadline.

Vesco, apparently a slow man to part with money, finally got around to withdrawing the cash from the Bahamas Commonwealth Bank in Nassau on April 6. The satchel full of hundred-dollar bills was brought to his Boonton, New Jersey, home. But for some undisclosed reason, which was not likely oversight, Vesco allowed the April 7 deadline to pass without turning the money over to Stans.

By April 10 he was ready to move. He had Laurence B. Richardson, Jr., president of International Controls Corporation, fly the briefcase stuffed with hundred-dollar greenbacks to Washington, where he delivered it to Stans. As he handed it over, he said lamely, "Sure hope that we might get some proper help somewhere along the line, if possible. . . ."

At this point he had confronted Stans with a criminal choice. The new law had been in effect for three days. It required the declaration of any contribution of over $100. When Stans placed the $200,000 in cash, plus a check for $50,000, in his office safe across the street from the White House, he was suggesting one of three things. He was either incredibly arrogant and did not believe the laws of the land applied to him, incredibly trusting and was willing to place his fate in the hands of one of the world's outsized manipulators, or he was incredibly stupid and will require a seeing eye dog to help him make his way around the jail cell he will most likely soon be occupying.

Under oath, Harry Sears described how rapidly the wheels moved now that they had been greased. At 1 P.M., two hours after Mr. Vesco became the largest single contributor of cash to the Nixon campaign, he was ushered into the presence of John Mitchell and informed him the money had been delivered. Within three hours Mitchell had paved the way for Sears to meet with SEC chairman William J. Casey, and his thirty-three year old counsel, G. Bradford Cook, soon to be the next chairman. Several additional meetings took place over the next few weeks, all devoted to Vesco's difficulties with the SEC.

Compounding Stans' failure to report the $200,000 to the General Accounting Office was his clumsy effort to cover up his blunder. As the SEC pressed on for an indictment of Vesco, the cornered financier used his credit with Stans. He bracketed each request for action with veiled threats, if such action was not forthcoming.

Stans consulted with Mitchell, and the former Attorney General contacted John Dean requesting he communicate with Chairman Casey. Dean was asked to obtain a postponement of the appearance of witnesses, perhaps in this manner shortcircuiting the SEC effort to indict Vesco.

As election day approached, Vesco was informing Stans that, unless the SEC was called off, he was going to reveal his still-secret donation. Meanwhile a harried Stans was scurrying around trying to keep the SEC from disclosing the very information Vesco was using to blackmail him.

While looking into the Vesco bank deposits, the SEC investigators had discovered the transfer of money from the Bahamas bank, and had concluded, because of hints dropped by Vesco associates, that the money had come to rest in Nixon's campaign headquarters.

On a goose hunt at Eagle's Lake, Texas, on November 13, Stans and SEC counsel Cook found themselves together on an open field. They had other geese to roast than those flying overhead. Cook told the Reuter's news agency that although they had been sitting fifteen yards from each other, "the goose-shooting was slow and we moved closer together."

A casual conversation was struck up. "Stans then asked me what I wanted to do—what my plans were," Cook recalled. "I said that Casey is going to be leaving, and he suggested that I make a run for the chairmanship."

Cook apparently thought it was about time that a thirty-five year old lawyer should become head of one of the government's most powerful agencies.

Continuing his discussion of job opportunities, Cook said he pleaded his case with Stans. He quoted Stans as saying, "I've heard some good things about you, blah, blah, blah."

When the blahing was over, Cook stated, "I brought up Vesco. He said that the SEC's 'massive' investigation had uncovered 'some cash which came in on a circular route.' Displaying his expertise, he said, 'It was a fairly good conjecture that it had been a political contribution.' "

To some it might seem peculiar that Counsel Cook should have brought up an investigatory matter with Nixon's finance chairman which might better have been pursued under oath in a court of law. However, Stans seemed to appreciate the opportunity to explore the subject under these more informal circumstances.

He wondered aloud whether it wouldn't be possible to eliminate from the commission's proposed suit mention of where Vesco's $200,000 in cash had ended up.

The grand jury later said Stans "asked Cook to limit the SEC inquiry . . . to facts concerning only the source and not the disposition of the money."

The SEC's final complaint was completely to Stans' satisfaction. It spoke vaguely of "large sums of cash" Vesco had moved, and concluded, "The source, ownership, use of, and accountability for, said monies are unknown."

Although Stans had his way with SEC, Vesco was not as easily put off. He could see that when it came to a matter of protecting Nixon's interests, Stans could work miracles with the SEC. However, the watchdog of corporate honesty continued to move its suit against him toward the courts.

In November, 1972, Vesco laid his last trump card on the table. He wrote a memorandum to Donald Nixon, the President's brother, as the grand jury charged, "the purport and tenor of which was to threaten disclosure of the secret cash contribution and other adverse consequences unless the SEC was directed to drop all legal proceeding against Vesco."

Although Mitchell had resigned as Chairman of the Committee for the Re-election of the President months earlier—apparently at the insistence of his wife Martha that he get out of "the dirty business" of politics— Vesco's memorandum somehow ended up on his desk. Mitchell, according to the grand jury, concealed its existence from the SEC and other law enforcement agencies "who properly should have been made aware of it."

Despite Mitchell and Stans' best efforts to extend the day of reckoning, the filing of the SEC suit on November 27 seeking to halt further plundering of Investors Overseas Services brought the matter to a head.

In January, 1973, the New York grand jury was convened to hear testimony from an "unidentified witness." U.S. Attorney Whitney North Seymour, Jr., began probing into the entire secret funds transaction. On Jan. 26 the *Washington Star-News,* which had been watching its rival, the *Post,* score all of the sensational newsbreaks on Watergate, reported that the government was looking into the donation.

On January 31, nine months after Vesco had set out his bait and three months after Nixon's landslide victory, Stans returned Vesco's $250,000. Unfortunately for Stans and Mitchell, it was nine months too late to be rejecting Vesco's obvious attempt at bribery.

On May 10, 1973 they were indicted on six counts

of perjury before the grand jury and three counts of obstructing justice. They faced jail sentences of up to fifty years.

Vesco and Sears were also indicted on one count of conspiracy and three counts of obstructing justice. Vesco was apparently so horrified at the thought he might have to spend twenty years in prison that he got into his four-engine jet and took off for Costa Rica, announcing he was planning to become a citizen of that banana republic.

This was an extraordinary event in American history for it was the first time two Cabinet officers had been indicted. In itself that is a remarkable testimony to the excellence of the American system established in Philadelphia in 1787. It speaks volumes for the sense of responsibility most men take with them when they enter the Presidential Cabinet.

However, it was a sad testimonial to the quality of the men with whom President Nixon had surrounded himself. Mitchell and Stans were not fringe members of the Cabinet. Mitchell, before his resignation in 1972 to take over as chairman of Nixon's campaign, was undoubtedly the most important member of the Cabinet. Stans had been an intimate of Nixon's going back to the Eisenhower Administration.

When young G. Bradford Cook resigned as head of the SEC on May 16, after seventy-four days in office, because of "the web of circumstances" his ambitions had involved him in with Stans, the realization was reenforced that the corrupting influences of money had reached into the top levels of the Nixon administration.

Each man might claim he had only the interests of Richard Nixon in mind when he betrayed his trust. But as Mitchell handed in his resignation as senior partner in Mudge, Rose, Guthrie, Alexander & Mitchell, and Stans issued a statement from The Committee for the Re-election of the President—which he still headed six months after its reason for existing seemed to have disappeared—a suspicion remained that both men knew the nature of their transgressions.

It was painful to remember Richard Nixon's acceptance speech to the Republican convention in 1968, as he spoke about the new day that would dawn when John Mitchell became chief law enforcement officer. "If we are going to restore order and respect for law in this country, there is one place we are going to begin: we are going to have a new Attorney General." The sham, sanctimony and self-deception that were to be hallmarks of the new administration were apparent in that homage.

# CHAPTER XI

## ... When First We Practice to Deceive

An enormous amount of the corrupt activities engaged in by Nixon's men occurred because of the need to raise large sums of money for his political campaigns. Men who work hard to accumulate fortunes are not likely to give money to strangers without the conviction they have bought something.

In many cases what they have bought is a ceremonial ambassador's post in some country where they would rarely think of spending a few days on vacation. Such people tenant the embassies in desert kingdoms, far off countries of the South Pacific, in fact most places in the underprivileged world from which their ancestors fled in desperation.

The qualifications for such posts are rarely facility with the country's language or a knowledge of its history and culture. It is merely the *desire* to have the title ambassador and the willingness to pay for it.

A review of the donation list to the 1972 Nixon campaign reveals some interesting examples. Henry Catto gave $25,000 and ended up in El Salvador, a Central American country dominated by mountains seldom under six thousand feet, whose neighbors are equally rocky Guatemala and Honduras. Anthony D. Marshall parted with $48,000 and was stationed in that garden spot of the Caribbean, Trinidad. John P. Humes was more generous, $100,000, and was more generously treated—Austria. Vincent P. de Roulet gave $29,000, while his wife's parents, multimillionaires Charles and Joan Whitney Payson, gave $86,000. He was given, in return, Jamaica.

The two gems, London and Paris, were contested hotly. W. Clement Stone, who wears collegiate bow ties and has many of the virtues of a self-made man, had poured money into Nixon campaigns for years. The seventy year old head of Combined Insurance Company of America had contributed approximately $4,100,000 for the 1968 and 1972 Nixon efforts. His major reward to date has been an invitation to Tricia's wedding. He wanted London or nothing and London went to Walter H. Annenberg, principal stockholder in Penn Central. Annenberg had contributed a mere $254,000.

Paris was passed on in regal fashion within the Watson family. Arthur K. Watson, who had embroiled himself in a *scandale* when he pressed money down a stewardess's cleavage on an inebriated flight over the Atlantic, had been the previous ambassador. Hundreds of thousands of dollars of the IBM fortune had been spent over the years in acquiring that position for him. To show that no hard feelings remained after the termination of his stewardship, he gave $300,000 in 1972, all before April 7, when disclosure could be avoided. His brother-in-law, John N. Irwin II, gave Nixon $50,000, and received the Paris appointment. It wasn't even necessary to move the family pictures out of the embassy.

Thomas Watson, brother of Arthur, and chairman of the executive committee of IBM, might also have helped swing Paris to Irwin. A lifelong Democrat, Thomas joined John Connally's Democrats for Nixon as vicechairman. That Irwin's advancement might not have been his sole motivation is suggested by the fact that the largest anti-trust action ever filed was pending against IBM.

Perhaps most bizarre was the payment to Nixon made by Ruth Lewis Farkas, wife of the owner of Alexander's department stores. Mrs. Farkas wanted to be ambassador to Luxembourg. In this endeavor, and undoubtedly out of affection for the President, she gave $300,000. But $250,000 of it was given to the committee *after* the election. Most of the money showed up in December, 1972, and January and February, 1973, in the form of $5,000 checks to various state Republican committees. This was a traditional method used to avoid the $5000 limitation on individual contributions in the Federal Corrupt Practices Act of 1925. One of John Dean's jobs in the White House had been to draw up the 450 charters for these bypasses to the law, most of which were merely mailing addresses.

The Farkas family fund for factional functionaries was largely contributed after the need for such funds was no longer apparent. Furthermore, it was placed in the treasury of Maurice Stans Finance Committee, which was already bloated with unused millions. Wyoming's Senator Gale McGee described Mrs. Farkas delayed payment as "a little unusual" and thought it would "probably delay" her confirmation.

The General Accounting Office reported that in 1972 President Nixon had received at least $1,300,000 from former and newly named ambassadors.

However, this practice had a certain air of innocence about it when compared to corporate donations, made with no thoughts of ceremonial appointments, invitations to White House prayer meetings, or pen and pencil sets inscribed with the President's signature.

One of the most glaring examples of the *quid pro quo* approach to contributions was the case of the ITT decision to funnel $400,000 to Nixon before the 1972 election. Harold Geneen, Chairman of the seven-billion-dollar international conglomerate, had supervised the acquisition of over one hundred companies during the previous ten years. He had pioneered in the creation of a new type of super-monopoly J. P. Morgan and Andrew Carnegie would have envied.

In his never-ending quest to find new enterprises to swallow up, Geneen had set his heart on subsidiarizing the Hartford Fire Insurance Company, one of the world's largest, and three smaller multimillion-dollar firms. The Justice Department's anti-trust division had been standing in his way since Lyndon Johnson's administration.

On August 4, 1970, Geneen decided the proper moment had come to clear the anti-trusters out of his way. He went to see their boss, Attorney General

Mitchell, and opened what one of the busiest Cabinet officers later described as "an entirely theoretical discussion about mergers."

On April 29, 1971, as Mitchell was increasingly involved in decisions about the building of Nixon's 1972 campaign apparatus, he arranged a meeting in his Justice Department office with Felix G. Rohatyn, ITT board member. After a short talk, Rohatyn was escorted downstairs by Peter M. Flanigan, White House aide on affairs concerning the business community, to deliver his "presentation" on the proposed merger to Richard McLaren, who was in charge of the case.

McLaren was bitterly opposed to the merger and had forcefully stated his opposition in a forty-eight-page memo submitted to Mitchell on February 24, 1971. However, arguments by Assistant Attorney General Kleindienst, Flanigan, and Rohatyn wore him down. He seemed to be convinced by talk about the "hardship" ITT would suffer if it was forced to divest itself of its acquisitions, and the possible "ripple effect" that might be suffered in the stock market.

Shortly after he gave his approval to the Hartford merger, McLaren was elevated to the Federal bench.

The matter might have rested there if President Nixon had not chosen Richard Kleindienst to succeed Mitchell as Attorney General; as a result, Kleindienst had been forced to seek Senate approval. In the midst of the hearings—which went on for weeks during the spring of 1972—as the Watergate burglars were perfecting their break-in plans, columnist Jack Anderson published a sensational memorandum written by Dita Beard.

Ms. Beard had been a bustling lobbiest for ITT for many years. She drank hard, laughed hard, and knew how to put the pressure on. Her utterly frank June 25, 1971 memo was addressed to William R. Merriam, head of ITT's Washington office. In it she spoke of ITT's "noble commitment" to give the Republican party $400,000 with which to stage its proposed 1972 San Diego convention.

She described the *noble commitment* as having "gone

a long way toward our negotiations on the mergers eventually coming out as Hal [Geneen] wants them. Certainly *the President has told Mitchell* to see that things are worked out fairly." [Italics added]

She spoke about her efforts in persuading Mitchell to get Nixon and others in the White House "on the higher level only" to bring pressure on McLaren. "It is still only McLaren's mickey-mouse we are suffering," she complained. Despite McLaren, she had few doubts about how matters would work out. "Mitchell is definitely helping us," she wrote confidently, and then concluded discreetly, "Please destroy this, huh?"

Merriam has no doubt wished many times he had followed her advice. And Richard Nixon has probably wished he had not finally pressed Kleindienst into the Attorney General's office, since less than a year later he was forced to accept his resignation at the height of the Watergate disclosures.

The contribution made by ITT was illegal. Corporations cannot make donations to political campaigns. Despite this violation of the law, the only penalty ITT had to suffer was to accept the return of its $400,000, tainted money with which Nixon was no longer willing to publicly be associated.

Richard Kleindienst's Justice Department could not bring itself to prosecute Richard Nixon's benefactor. That was the central point in this not so subtle attempt at "higher level" institutional bribery. The *quid* in the affair was ITT, but the *quo* was the President of the United States. He was to be the candidate at San Diego. There was no other serious contender. He was the person for whom the convention was being staged. He was going to be the only person, aside from the "higher levels" of ITT, who received any direct benefit from the conglomerate's $400,000.

That men seeking favors from the Nixon administration would make their way to the offices of the country's chief law enforcement agent, had apparently become common knowledge. In late 1970 Robert T. Carson, administrative assistant to Senator Hiram L. Fong, Republican of Hawaii, visited with Deputy Attorney General Kleindienst. His sole topic of conversation was the discussion of a possible $100,000 contribution to the President's reelection campaign *if* certain indictments being sought by the Justice Department and the SEC could be squashed.

Kleindienst did not seem shocked that such a suggestion should be made. He said later that he did not initially consider the discussion a bribe offer. Well, then, what made him change his mind and view this matter as any honest citizen might?

Approximately a week after the visit, FBI agents sought permission from Kleindienst and Mitchell to conduct electronic surveillance on the generous Carson. Suddenly Kleindienst realized he had been the target of a bribery attempt. His report was added to the FBI's record. Thereupon the sixty-six year old Carson was convicted of conspiracy and lying to a grand jury, and sent to prison for eighteen months. In such ways are the wicked in the lower levels of government punished.

In fact, matters had gotten to the point where, on October 23, 1972, a Houston oilman was willing to tell *Time* Magazine about his motive in giving a large donation to Nixon. "Can the guy who gave the President $20,000 pick up the phone and call the White House if he gets into trouble with the feds? You bet. Does he realize this when he gives? You bet."

Texas millionaires have understood this eleemosynary rule of the thumb for decades, going back to the passage of the Oil Depletion Allowance in the 1920's. No more aware Texan lived than Robert H. Allen, chairman of the Texas Finance Committee to Re-elect the President and a president in his own rights, of the Gulf Resources & Chemical Company.

In early 1972 Allen either raised or donated out of his own pocket $100,000. He deposited it in the accounts of Gulf Resources & Chemical, perhaps an injudicious move on his part. For it must be remembered that corporations are not allowed to contribute to political campaigns.

On April 3, Allen triggered a startling series of transactions. By phone, he had the $100,000 transferred to Compania de Azufre Veracruz in Mexico city. Azufre Veracruz was a subsidiary of Gulf, but was almost entirely inactive. The money was quickly withdrawn by attorney Manuel Ogarrio Daguerre, not having spent enough time in the Mexican bank to earn a penny's interest.

Daguerre handed the money, in the form of $89,000 in bank drafts and $11,000 in hundred-dollar bills, to an unidentified messenger, who transported it back to Houston on April 5. In the trade, this is called a "laundering job." Money, possibly soiled with unimaginable stains, had gone off to Mexico and come back different, and yet the same—but most important, unidentifiable.

In Houston, Allen added $600,000 raised from other sources to a suitcase containing the Mexican money and sent it off on a Pennzoil plane to Washington. The president of Pennzoil was William C. Liedtke, Jr., Nixon fund raiser in the Southwest. The money was from anonymous sources and was being sent to Stans before the April 7 deadline on disclosure. Roy Winchester, Pennzoil lobbyist, was the delivery man. When he reached Washington that night, he went directly to 1701 Pennsylvania Avenue and the money was deposited in Maurice Stans's safe.

At least some Republicans were trying to respond to Stans's request that they donate at least one percent of their gross income. As he reminded them in 1972, "that's a low price to pay every four years to ensure that the Executive branch of government is in the right hands."

The General Accounting Office, which is the auditing arm of Congress, eventually determined that up to $700,000 in undeclared money was at one time or another kept in Stans's safe. Vesco's $200,000 in cash was secreted there.

Snuggling among the rest of the laundered bills was $25,000 from Dwayne O. Andreas, a Minneapolis millionaire. Andreas preferred Democrats; or at least his

$75,000 donation to Hubert Humphrey's primary campaign earlier in the year suggests that he did

Andreas had given his Republican $25,000 to Kenneth H. Dahlberg, Nixon's Midwest finance chief. Andreas and Dahlberg were members of a group which applied for a federal bank charter soon after the money came to rest in Stans's safe. Those of suspicious natures will find something to sniff at because of the 424 applications for such charters since 1966, only twelve received more rapid approval.

The Andreas money did not arrive at the office of the Finance Committee for the Re-election of the President until April 9, two days after the deadline. It remained undeclared, sharing that criminal distinction with the $89,000 from Mexico.

The combined $114,000 was now taken to Miami by G. Gordon Liddy, officially counsel to the Finance Committee, where it was deposited in Bernard Barker's account. The next time the money surfaced was in the Democratic headquarters at the Watergate, where it was found in the pockets of Barker and his fellow burglars.

It is understandable why such a great effort was made to hide the sources of the two contributions that eventually paid for the break-in, for there is no indication that either Robert Allen or Dwayne Andreas thought their money was going to be spent on anything except posters, advertising and other legitimate campaign expenses. After the Justice Department revealed it was making a criminal investigation in January, 1973, Allen asked for, and received, a refund of his money. Andreas's money was also returned.

The premeditated care taken by the men who were soliciting this $114,000 to divorce the source of the money from its eventual users is equally clear. There is in this deceit room for conjecture that the men who routed this money into and out of Stans's safe were involved in decisions on how that money was to be used.

There was still $350,000 left in Stans's safe. It was

soon taken and deposited in a Washington bank. The deposit slip bore the notation, "Cash on hand to 4/7/72 from 1968 campaign." Stans claimed later to GAO investigators that the notation was fraudulent. At least some of the money was of a more recent vintage.

Attorney General Kleindienst had pointed out the nature of the crime when he said that disclosure of campaign financing was "the essence of our democratic processes."

The dimensions of the hidden funds did not begin to be seen until after the election. In April, 1973, as the Watergate scandal was beginning to drive all other news off the front pages, it was revealed H. R. Haldeman had another secret cache of $350,000 in his safe in the White House. A third secret fund of at least $500,000 was controlled by Kalmbach, and financed West Coast operations, such as Donald Segretti's shenanigans.

On May 19, 1973, the GAO issued a new report, more condemning in tone, in which it revealed that Kalmbach had at one time in 1972 held $1,900,000 in Republican cash. Of this previously undisclosed amount, $1,650,000 had been left over from the 1968 campaign. Stans had given Kalmbach $250,000 to augment the funds lying around since 1968.

The GAO cited other previously unrecorded Kalmbach campaign financial dealings, but reserved particularly harsh comment for his activities in the summer of 1972, immediately after the Watergate break-in.

A cash contribution of $75,000 was delivered to Kalmbach on June 29, six weeks after the April 7 mandatory disclosure deadline, and never reported. The money was from Thomas V. Jones, president of the California based Northrop Corporation, one of the government's aerospace contractors.

The GAO alleged that the $75,000 became part of the $230,000 Nixon's personal attorney solicited—and received—during the summer of 1972, which was then distributed to the Watergate burglars and their attorneys.

It may be wondered, as information is uncovered and

distance adds perspective, why men like Kalmbach, Stans and others of standing in the Republican hierarchy felt compelled to supply burglars, caught in the execution of a felony, with sizable amounts of money. There is such an awful suggestion of complicity in this act that their continued ability to proclaim their innocence remains the true measure of their shamelessness.

Much of the information the GAO forwarded to the Justice Department for action was obtained from Hugh W. Sloan, Jr., the treasurer of Stans's finance committee. Sloan had been only twenty-seven when he went to work for the 1968 Nixon campaign as assistant finance director. After the inauguration, youthful Sloan, motivated by admiration and bedazzled by the scene spread out before him, was added to the White House staff, working for Dwight L. Chapin, Nixon's appointments secretary. In this capacity Sloan was considered part of the Haldeman cabal, although no more than a soldier in the ranks.

In March, 1971, he followed Murray Chotiner out of the White House and helped construct the financial machinery for the campaign. By February, 1972, he was treasurer, and in that role signed for the disbursement of funds. Sloan actually handed Liddy the cash to be used in the Watergate break-in.

Shortly after the burglars were captured and Sloan realized what had been going on under his nose during all these months, he resigned and began speaking to grand juries and whoever else would listen to him. His most impressive charge was that he had been urged by Nixon officials to commit perjury when questioned about disbursements by the grand jury. John Mitchell's cryptic advice to him, when he sought guidance in a pending interview with the FBI investigators was, "When the going gets tough, the tough get going." Such banalities did not quiet his agitation.

His description of the scene in the innermost recesses of the White House was illuminating.

"There was no independent sense of morality there. I mean if you worked for someone, he was God and whatever the orders were, you did it—and there were damned few who were able to make, or willing to make, independent judgments.

"It was all so narrow, so closed. Nobody listened to anybody who wasn't in a superior position. They were guys who had committed themselves economically to politics—you know, in a way in which it was not only what they were doing at the moment but what they were going to be doing all their lives, and because of that there emerged some kind of separate morality about things."

The out-of-control ambitions of these men, confronted with the need for private sources of wealth to make possible the realization of those ambitions, was a cause of their "separate morality." It is under those circumstances that men in control of enormous quantities of money wield their power most effectively. They do not yearn for the notoriety of political life, the acclaim of public recognition. But those who do must come to them.

In the process a price is extracted and the horror of the bargain is that the American people pay the cost in higher taxes and a lower standard of living. For the President is now in a position to grant favors to companies and individuals that change the lives of citizens within the privacy of their home. By allowing the meat packers to raise their prices, he determines how much meat a housewife may place before her family. By allowing the oil industry to raise the price of fuel oil, he determines whether some families will be able to live in comfort through a cold winter.

His economic grip over the country is so complete that a decision on import quotas, farm subsidy payments, limitations on pay increases, wiping out of rent controls can help create inflation. The 1972 election demonstrated that too many of these decisions were based on personal obligations the President of the United States owed to men who saw a profit in supplying him with $50,000,000.

# Chapter XII

## *Watergate*

"When I am the candidate," President Nixon told a television interviewer in early 1971, "I run the campaign."

The fact that he did run the 1972 campaign exactly as he had predicted is confirmed by Jeb Stuart Magruder, one of Haldeman's closest White House aides, who was temporary chairman of the Committee for the Re-election of the President until John Mitchell was ready to officially take over March, 1972, when Magruder became deputy chairman.

"There was basically a triad of senior decision makers," he told a Harvard University seminar in January, 1973. "The President, Bob Haldeman and John Mitchell. . . . They were in constant consultation with each other over major activities."

But Magruder's testimony is not needed on this matter. Richard Nixon had never in his life entrusted an electoral contest to the whimsy of other men. In fact, he had always displayed a compulsive need to control even the most insignificant details.

When campaigning, nothing else mattered; food, family, sleep, all went by the board. It was as though he were in a struggle for life itself, and in that kind of struggle very few holds were barred.

The motif of his political career has been, prepare for the next election. In preparation for the 1968 and 1972 campaigns he gathered around him an extraordinarily youthful group of men, all of whom could remain only as long as they accepted the principle that the election of Richard Nixon was the most important national goal of true Americans.

In that reverential atmosphere, many acts were undertaken which were probably uncharacteristic of some of the men involved. Early in the first Nixon administration it was considered acceptable to suspect the President's opponents of such evil intent and such potentially malicious, damaging behavior that methods of operation came into ordinary use that had rarely been used before.

Critical reporters were not merely berated by Vice-President Agnew; their phones were tapped by the FBI and investigations were made into their backgrounds. In 1971, CBS correspondent Daniel Schorr was the subject of an FBI profile as a result of Haldeman's personal orders—an action that later called for a personal apology.

Radical youth groups with infinitesimal support were infiltrated. *Agent provocateurs* primed them for violence, often leading them into confrontations with the police in front of television cameras. In Camden, New Jersey, a government agent planned and directed the destruction of draft records.

In the process of maintaining Richard Nixon in office, the Secret Service, the FBI and the CIA, each of which had been traditionally disengaged from politics, each of which was a potential instrument for excess, were used as tools for his aggrandizement.

No doubt the men employed in this manner thought of themselves as patriots. The subtleties of genuine democratic practice often escape the vision of the grim advocate.

Nixon's statement at the beginning of his administration that what he planned to do was to "bring the nation together" was clearly never the guideline of his actions. Instead John Mitchell's cautioning to Americans, "Watch what we do, not what we say," became the most honest expression of the Nixon ethic.

Too much of Nixon's adult life was spent dividing people, leading them into fights against each other, questioning their motives, challenging their right to speak. As President he did not change this mode of behavior, he was merely given a new setting in which to act. Rather than being the leader of all Americans, a point of inspiration and a noble example, he became the leader of a small group of callow adherents who tended to view everyone not in their circle as inferiors who were a potential threat, and against whom measures had to be taken. At best, they viewed Americans as boobs who had to be spoken to infrequently and with infinite care. The most effective method of speaking to them was with slogans, and the least effective was to employ the full truth.

Haldeman was not merely a technician, shuffling papers and making sure every empty desk in the White House had someone sitting behind it. He was a man of convictions, the most important of which were molded by an élitist view of life. The campaign slogans he approved were "Nixon Now" and "Four More Years," neither one of which provoked a single thought beyond the reelection of someone he decided must be described as "The President."

Is it any wonder the campaign developed as it did? Approval had to be garnered from that large mass of the unwashed who somehow had managed to gain the right to vote. This attitude was not merely a display of skepticism about people. It was an absolute conviction that they could not be trusted to find their way to the shrine at which Haldeman worshipped.

The Harris poll released in May, 1971, which showed Senator Muskie leading the President by a 47 to 39 per centage, tipped the balance in favor of panic. A strategem of pulling down Muskie and Kennedy, while building up George Wallace and McGovern was set into motion. The chief tool was to be sabotage.

By July, Hunt and Liddy were already on the scene. All summer they were bugging phones and trying to hire a government worker to spy on Kennedy, even while Murray Chotiner was assuring me, on August 5, in his Reeves & Harrison office, that "the President feels his weakest possible opponent would be Teddy Kennedy."

At that very moment Hunt and Liddy were across

the street in Room 16 of the Executive Office Building planning the burglary of Ellsberg's psychiatrist's office.

During the next month work began on the forging of the Diem cables. In September James W. McCord, Jr., one of the seven caught at Watergate, was hired by the reelection committee as a "security consultant."

The sabotage apparatus took shape that month when Donald Segretti, twenty-six, was hired by White House appointments secretary Dwight Chapin, thirty, with the approval of Haldeman, to spy on Democratic candidates and disrupt their campaigns.

Segretti then travelled widely in an attempt to recruit a number of agents who would infiltrate into the camp of each of the Democratic candidates.

On December 10, Magruder, now in charge of the Committee for the Re-election of the President, hired Liddy as the committee's counsel. Until the moment Haldeman authorized his transfer, Liddy was on a government payroll and his crimes were paid for by American taxpayers. After December 10 his lawbreaking was paid for out of funds contributed by Republicans who thought they were taking part in a normal democratic process.

From the first, Liddy's purpose at the committee was clear. He was in charge of McCord, who was a retired CIA agent with twenty years' knowledge of bugging, wiretapping and clandestine photography. McCord was also a puritan at heart, a family man and a church-goer.

On May 18, 1973, McCord told the Senate Select Committee on Presidential Campaign Activities, which was investigating the Watergate case, that as soon as the persuasive Liddy arrived, his simple task of checking the locks on windows and doors, watching visitors, and responding to any request for bodyguard services, changed.

"The discussions in December, January, February of [1971 and] 1972 with Mr. Liddy, gradually developed into more and more conversation on his part with me in the offices of the Committee for the Re-election of the President regarding the technical devices and political matters pertaining to the forthcoming convention . . ."

McCord spoke with pride from his storehouse of knowledge. But as time passed it "became apparent that he [Liddy] had an interest in several areas of intelligence gathering pertaining to the Democratic party and the Democratic convention, and in which it was contemplated or planned by him and by others whom he referred to in these conversations as John Mitchell, John Dean, counsel to the President, [and] Jeb Magruder . . . in which it appeared that those men . . . by late January [were in the] . . . planning stage in which political intelligence was to be discussed at meetings at the Attorney General's office . . . and in which Mr. Liddy was seeking from me certain information regarding the costs and the types of electronic devices that could be used in bugging."

That Liddy's interests covered a broader field of activity is revealed by McCord's comment: "The second part dealt with photography operations, clandestine photography operations, and a third part dealt with the broad area of political espionage, political intelligence."

On January 24, 1972, Liddy took his preliminary plans for the break-in to John Mitchell's office in the Justice Department. At this time Mitchell was still the Attorney General, whose main duty it was to enforce the law. Yet he sat listening to Liddy, in the presence of Jeb Magruder and John Dean, trying to make up his mind whether to authorize a criminal act against a political opponent. The Democratic Party headquarters in the Watergate could by no stretch of the imagination be considered a subversive nest, nurturing in it numerous threats to "national security." The only people there were rivals he wanted to beat in the November election.

Yet he sat there pondering whether Liddy's plans made it a risk worth taking. At his side, in the form of John Dean, was the President's counsel, apparently sent from the White House to find out exactly what was going on.

It was a scene out of an Elizabethan melodrama, with a cast of practical men, some of whom may have thought they were inspired by good motives, but all of whom were willing to do what had to be done.

Liddy was encouraged at that meeting to do some more homework, and to return on February 4. In preparation for the new meeting, Liddy had an elaborate set of charts drawn up. It was a full-scale, diagrammatical presentation which would have made any advertising executive proud. It cost $7,000 and helped convince McCord anything that expensive must have been approved by men in authority.

On February 4 Liddy presented his charts to the same group of men in Mitchell's office. He also presented a budget proposal. McCord said, "I saw it [the budget proposal] in writing, in a draft on his [Liddy's] desk on one occasion and in a typed memorandum on a second occasion. [It was] approximately $450,000."

McCord testified that thirty days later, after Mitchell had mulled over the plan, a budget of $250,000 was approved, and the go-ahead was given.

Why had McCord, convicted only of traffic violations, allowed himself to take part in such a transparently illegal activity?

"The decision process, I think, on my part," he said in the deliberate tones of a man who had agonized over that question, "took place after the thirty-day delay . . . in which it appeared that this whole matter was being considered, reconsidered, discussed and so on by Mr. Mitchell. It was also very material to me that he had considered it while in the Attorney General's office."

Liddy exploited this purported relationship with Mitchell skillfully. "Sometimes he would tell me," McCord said, "I am getting ready to go up to see the Attorney General to discuss this operation, referring to the Watergate operation . . . Sometimes he would tell me, I have just come back from that operation, concluding what we are going to do now."

There was an aura of respectability built up around

this felony which lulled the law-and-order sensibilities of this upright man. "The evidence that the counsel to the President sat in with him," he explained, "on the meetings of this and, therefore, both the White House was represented and the Attorney General of the United States were represented in this decision and that this thirty-day delay to me, I drew the conclusion that the Attorney General himself had conveyed the decision to his own superior for final decision." He also asserted he believed the Attorney General "has the power to make illegal matters legal with the stroke of a pen."

Once convinced, McCord vigorously joined in the conspiracy. During February, 1972, he and Liddy rented space in 1908 K Street, the building next to Senator Muskie's Washington headquarters. The plan was to bug Muskie's phone—a pre-Watergate practice session. McCord used his name on the lease but Liddy wrote down one of his aliases, John B. Hayes.

It was a month of geared-up political activity for the Nixon campaign. Mitchell resigned on February 15, the resignation to take effect on March 1. Maurice Stans left his post as Secretary of Commerce and took over the last few weeks of the crunch-drive to get as much undeclared money as he could before the April 7 deadline. Liddy and Hunt flew down to Miami for a meeting with Segretti, a meeting arranged by Haldeman. At this meeting Haldeman reduced his role over Segretti to that of a monitor, while Liddy and Hunt were given more direct responsibility for the sabotage campaign.

The key meetings in the Watergate intrigue were held on March 4 and 5 at Richard Nixon's Key Biscayne home. Present were Mitchell, now officially in command of the campaign, Magruder, Liddy and Fred LeRue, Mitchell's trusted aide.

Mitchell agrees that the meeting took place, but claims he vetoed the plan. What he was admitting, incredible as it may seem, was that as Attorney General he had listened as men about him planned a criminal act, and had not reported them to the authorities. Furthermore he had listened to them repeatedly, not once raising his hand to say he did not want to hear another word. Indeed, he had entertained these criminals in the President's house, encouraging them by this very act to assume Nixon himself was willing to tolerate, if not condone, what they were planning.

On April 1, Liddy was transferred from CRP to the Finance Committee for CRP where he worked directly under Maurice Stans. As disclosure day approached, campaign headquarters began to have a "madhouse" atmosphere, according to Sally J. Harmony, Liddy's secretary. Money was coming in from all over the world.

Hugh Sloan revealed in 520 pages of testimony taken in a suit by the public interest group *Common Cause,* which was suing for full disclosure of Nixon campaign finances, that one to two million dollars in cash, on which no records were kept, was on hand as the April 7 deadline approached.

Common Cause attorneys, who had received court permission to review Nixon campaign financial records, stated that although the committee had reported having $10,200,000 on April 7, it actually had $22,000,000, leaving $11,800,000 unaccounted for either as to who donated it, or how it was dispensed.

Sloan said, "At Secretary Stans's instruction I personally destroyed the working copy . . . and turned the summary sheet over to the secretary. I have since been led to understand that that has been destroyed."

There was in this undeclared, unaccounted for treasury enough money to bribe an army of honest men. Yet any sign of its existence had been reduced to dust in the giant shredding machine which had become such a vital part of the office routine at 1701.

Sloan also reported he gave Gordon Strachan $350,-000 in a little black bag which was taken to Haldeman's White House safe. Liddy was given approximately $300,000 in hundred-dollar bills with which to bankroll the far-flung espionage and sabotage efforts.

Liddy was now operating on a level that must have given him great satisfaction. There was enough plotting and intriguing to satisfy a dozen Iagos. Sometime in April, Jack Anderson reported, Liddy tried to buy some guns. The Virginia gun dealer, to whom Liddy nervously showed his White House credentials, claimed he wanted to purchase "a small arsenal" of pistols. However, the dealer had recently gotten into trouble because he had sold anti-tank guns to a man who used one to rob a Brink's vault.

Besides, the dealer recalled, "There was something wrong about him. You know, he acted a little flaky."

The dealer refused to sell Liddy the five to ten pistols he wanted and reported the incident to the Treasury Department's gun-control unit. According to the dealer, an official of the unit verified that Liddy held a White House pass. He was left with the strong impression Liddy wanted the guns for associates of his involved in a mutual venture.

On May 2 the Cuban contingent, which was soon to be rousting through Democratic headquarters, became involved in the disruption of a Daniel Ellsberg anti-war rally. They claim they were told it was a CIA operation. Ellsberg was to be roughed up and anti-Communist slogans were to be shouted as they ran off. The incident, which almost seems to have been staged in order to bring the Watergate team to peak form, was a fiasco. Ellsberg was scarcely bumped. Those in charge of the break-in might well have considered the lessons of the May 2 action and revised their approach to campaigning.

Instead they drove on relentlessly, thinking perhaps the thought so colorfully expressed by Charles Colson months later: "The charge of subverting the whole political process is a fantasy, a work of fiction rivaling only *Gone With the Wind* in circulation and *Portnoy's Complaint* for indecency."

On May 8 Bernard Barker, key figure in the Watergate break-in, withdrew the $114,000 Nixon campaign money, which had been largely laundered in Mexico. He alerted his Cuban friends that another "CIA mission" for America's national security, which would at the same time be a blow against Fidel Castro, was coming up soon.

A steady round of meetings now took place between Liddy and Hunt, often with Magruder, occasionally with Mitchell, all pointing toward an early break-in to the Watergate. According to McCord, Mitchell decided on "priorities." First of all, a tap must be placed on Democratic National Chairman Larry O'Brien's phone. A second tap should be placed on the phone of any other top official of the DNC.

McCord, still going through the motions of being the security officer for CRP, nevertheless found time to perform some tasks for Liddy, for which services he was getting an additional $2,000 per month "hazard pay." In an endeavor to find additional hands, he phoned Alfred Baldwin III in New York and asked him if he was interested in a security job. Baldwin, a former FBI agent down on his luck, was shortly to be the lookout man in the Howard Johnson motel across the street from the Watergate.

When he arrived in Washington the next day, McCord took him to see Fred LaRue, Mitchell's surrogate. LaRue approved, and Baldwin was supplied with a .38 caliber pistol.

During the rest of May, McCord collected devices which would be used to bug the Watergate. His major additional responsibility was to pick up FBI reports and other intelligence information from the Internal Security Division of the Justice Department. He later informed the Erwin Committee that at least one of the reports was on McGovern's political activity. McCord's access to the reports was authorized, he claimed, after he wrote a memo to John Mitchell requesting permission, although Mitchell no longer had any official connection with the Justice Department.

On May 24, the burglary team was brought together at a Washington hotel for a briefing. Liddy announced that Barker was to be the "team captain" for the first break-in. This was the first time McCord met him or the other three Cuban-Americans. McCord's comment: "I liked Mr. Barker. . . . He was reliable and dependable."

In the meanwhile, the man for whom all this was being done was arriving in Moscow on May 22. This was the follow-up to his successful February trip to Peking, and was the major cause for the rise in his popularity which had been showing up in recent polls. While he was toasting Brezhnev, the Liddy-Hunt gang was making the first two unsuccessful attempts to break into the Democrats headquarters at Watergate.

At the end of May, while everyone was away enjoying the Memorial Day weekend, the burglars made their third attempt. McCord described their functions to the Erwin Committee in a detached, professional manner:

"Mr. Liddy was in overall charge of the operation. Mr. Hunt was his assistant. Mr. Barker was the team captain of the group going in. My job was that of the electronic installation, and the others of the group—the other Cuban-Americans—had functions divided into two categories: one of photographing certain documents within the committee; a couple of men had the function of generally being lookouts while we were inside."

The mission was accomplished. The taps were placed on O'Brien's phone and the phone of Spencer Oliver, executive director of the Democratic National Committee, whose responsibility it was to keep in touch with state chairman throughout the nation.

From the start there was something wrong with the Oliver tap. However, O'Brien's phone was a cornucopia of constantly flowing information. His conversations were recorded by Alfred Baldwin at a listening station across the street in the Howard Johnson Motel. They were then taken to Liddy's office in the Finance Committee, where his secretary, Sally Harmony, would type them out and sent transcripts on to Jeb Magruder. This was the notorious "Gemstone" file.

Had Mitchell been satisfied with the golden O'Brien voice and the tacky "secrets" being fed into his ear, it is entirely possible the mammoth job of uncovering the tangled details of the Republican electoral conspiracy would never have been undertaken.

But there was a striving for perfection among Nixon's servants, and Oliver's malfunctioning tap provoked them into planning the fatal fourth intrusion. McCord described their reasoning:

"Mr. Liddy had told me that Mr. Mitchell . . . liked the 'takes'; that is, the documents that had been photographed on the first entry . . . and that he wanted a second photographic operation to take place, and that, in addition, as long as that team was going in, that Mr. Mitchell wanted, had passed instructions to Mr. Liddy, to check to see what the malfunctioning of the second device . . . was."

But there was to be one major expansion of the technology applied the second time around. "He [Liddy] also said Mr. Mitchell wanted a room bug as opposed to a device on a telephone installed in Mr. O'Brien's office itself in order to transmit not only telephone conversations but conversations out of the room itself, beyond whatever might be spoken on the telephone."

In such ways do men overreach themselves.

On Friday afternoon, June 16, 1972, four Cuban anti-Castro refugees led by Bernard Barker took off from Miami airport on Eastern Airlines Flight 190. They landed at Washington National Airport at 3:59, where Barker used an American Express card to rent a car.

Barker, fifty-five, had helped E. Howard Hunt organize the 1961 Bay of Pigs invasion against Castro. At that time he had been known as *Macho* and Hunt used the code name *Eduardo*. Once in Washington, Barker rented rooms 214 and 314 at the Watergate Hotel. With him were Frank Stugis, forty eight, Eugenio R. Martinez, fifty one; and Virgilio R. Gonzalez, forty five, a locksmith. They dined on lobster in the hotel restaurant and then spent the rest of the evening getting last-minute instructions from Liddy and Hunt, and preparing their equipment.

They carried with them two 35-mm cameras fitted

with close-up lens attachments. They had forty rolls of film and a high-intensity lamp. McCord had microphones and transmitters which were to be installed in the ceiling of O'Brien's office. There was also an assortment of lock picks and burglary tools, two walkie-talkies, with which to maintain contact with lookout Alfred Baldwin, once again stationed in the Howard Johnson motel so that he could watch the entrance to the Watergate Office Building.

They prepared to carry several cans of tear gas and pen-like containers of mace. Each of them was given a pair of rubber surgical gloves. They were dressed neatly in businessmen's suits. Barker pocketed $5,300 in hundred-dollar bills with which to defray any incidental expenses arising from the Washington trip.

Shortly before midnight, accompanied by McCord, they parted from Liddy and Hunt. The Watergate Hotel and Office Building are separate entities within the Watergate complex and are connected through a basement garage. The locks on the doors of two basement stairwells were taped by McCord so that the tongue mechanism in the door could not thrust into the groove in the door frame.

As they prepared to enter the stairwell, Frank Wills, a poorly paid security guard who had just come on the midnight-to-7 A.M. shift, made his first rounds. He turned the knob on the door at the B2 level and discovered the lock had been tampered with. "I took the tape off but I didn't think anything of it. I thought maybe the building's engineer had done it."

After removing the tapes, Wills went on about his duties. When the five interlopers discovered their tapes had been removed, they panicked. They returned to the area below the Watergate Restaurant; there it was decided that the locksmith Gonzalez would go back and pick the locks, while Barker was sent up to Liddy and Hunt to discuss the possibility of calling off the break-in. McCord went to the motel to await word. Liddy sent Barker back with word not to worry and the mission was on.

In the meanwhile, Gonzalez and a companion had retaped the latches and, in fact, had left their calling card at several other stairwell doorways. The intrusion was set in motion just prior to 12:30 A.M. on June 17.

Shortly after that, Wills, apparently uncomfortable at the thought of what he had found, returned to the doors and discovered new tapes. "It seemed mighty suspicious, it being on there again that quick," he remarked later.

Although Wills says he made his second round at 12:30, his call to Second District headquarters was not logged until 1:52. The first call to investigate a possible burglary at the Watergate Office Building did not go out until after 2. A first attempt to assign a uniformed policeman in a clearly marked patrol car failed. He was out of gas. Then three tactical patrolmen wearing street clothes and riding in an unmarked car were sent to check what was proving to be an extremely unhurried burglary. They were Sgt. Paul Leper and Officers John Barrett and Carl Shollfer.

Baldwin noticed the three casually dressed men enter the building, but his anxiety was not aroused. After a few minutes he tried to call over the news that three men were now on the balconies of the sixth floor. His warning to the intruders, now fascinated with the work they had been doing for two hours, did not break their concentration. Their walkie-talkie was off. Suddenly Baldwin heard McCord's whispered voice: "They've got us."

The three policemen who worked their way down from the eighth floor, where they discovered the first taped latch, to the offices of Democratic National headquarters on the sixth floor, were not prepared for what they found.

The Watergate complex had been the target for many robberies. It was the dwelling place of three Cabinet officers and numerous wealthy people, who enjoyed being in the heart of Washington, yet having the pleasure of a Potomac view, and the esthetic convenience of being across the street from the Kennedy Center For the Performing Arts.

The men who came to rob the Watergate were looking for jewels and money. Whatever else they settled for was easily converted into cash. Yet here were five distinguished looking men cowering behind desks as the police flashlights picked around the room. As they obeyed orders and lined up against the wall, their surgical gloves suddenly in view over their heads, the scene became steadily more bizarre. Two panels were ripped out of the office roof. Files lay in disarray. Random damage had been done all over the suite. It is clear that, if they had gone undetected, the burglers would have had to spend a great deal more time straightening up their mess, so as not to arouse the suspicions of the staff when they returned on Monday morning. Any sign of forced entry would have probably led to a search, which would have uncovered the bugs in the ceiling and the taps on the phones.

The five felons were now led away to the D.C. jail, as Alfred Baldwin III pressed the panic button to alert Liddy and Hunt that something had gone wrong. They fled from their hotel room in terror at the thought of what was about to occur. Perhaps Liddy had a moment to wonder what might have happened if only that Virginia gun dealer had not been so suspicious.

# Chapter XIII

## *The Cover-Up*

Had the crimes of the Nixon Administration ended with Watergate, there would have been enough evil committed to label it one of the most corrupt in history. However, there were crimes that proceeded from the clumsy, pre-doomed efforts to hide the White House staff's direction of the massive burglary, sabotage, spying and campaign fund illegalities. These new exertions entrangled large numbers of additional people. Their careers and lives were casually gambled with in an endeavor to save a handful of egocentric men clustered around the President.

Finally enmeshed in the plot were dozens of men, from obscure retired New York City police officers to the most intimate associates of the President. Included was every top official of the 1972 Nixon reelection campaign, all of whom had been transferred from the upper echelons of the White House staff. Invariably these men led upright private lives. Most of them were abstainers. Few of them smoked. Almost everyone of them had a solid relationship with some local church. Yet each of them participated in serious crimes, many of which they initiated, all of which they took part in with relish. Their major concern seemed to be, how could the President's desires be most rapidly and completely carried out? Only a Nero could have fully appreciated their efforts.

These men held loyalty to Richard Nixon above loyalty to American institutions. Incensed with their proximity to power and their conviction that Nixon's reelection was vital to the nation's survival, they came to consider themselves above the law.

When finally exposed many excused themselves by saying that their orders had come from higher up, from either Attorney General Mitchell, Haldeman, Ehrlich-man, or Dean; and therefore they assumed the proposed crime had the sanction of the President.

That inferred sanction was enough to make most of them willing to violate their oath to uphold the Consti-tution and the laws of the land. It was not true of all of them, but it was almost invariably true of the men closest to the President, those that he had most person-ally selected.

The attempt to cover up the true nature of the crime and White House involvement began as soon as the burglars were booked. They gave false names and re-fused to answer questions. Within minutes after their arrest, two lawyers, Douglas Caddy and a Mr. Raffety, unknown to them, appeared at the jailhouse and repre-sented themselves as their counsels. They were sent by Hunt and Liddy and advised the arrested men to remain silent, help was on the way.

Word of the arrests spread quickly, but except for those informed by Hunt and Liddy, the identity of the burglars remained a secret most of the day. Robert C. Odle, twenty-eight, office manager of CRP, who previ-ously thought McCord was working solely under his direction, told the Ervin Committee of his immediate comment to the person giving him the news of the burg-lary: "That could never happen here," he said with a barely suppressed touch of youthful glee, "because I have this guy working for me, Jim McCord . . . (laugh-ter) and he has this place tight."

Odle shortly discovered his guy McCord was one of the five thieves. Late in the afternoon, while still trying to absorb this shocking news, he received a California call from Jeb Magruder, the man who was sending transcriptions of O'Brien's taps to Mitchell. After dis-cussing McCord's arrest, Magruder said that he was worried and wanted certain things of his taken out of his desk and out of the office. Odle identified the main cause of concern as what he called "the strategy file," which he accommodatingly took home with him. In fact, this was the blue "Gemstone" file, whose security, under these circumstances, was of prime concern to Magruder.

Gordon Stachan, according to Odle, was all over the place. "Strachan was Haldeman's eyes and ears with the Committee," he said. Another peripatetic individual was Gordon Liddy.

Odle saw Liddy in the third floor hall looking around in puzzlement. When he caught sight of Odle, he asked where the "big" paper shredder was. Although news of the crime was on everyone's lips, the office manager's curiosity was not in the slightest aroused. He pointed to the shredding room. Liddy, in the possession of "a stack of foot-high documents," then asked how to work the machine. Odle, always helpful, responded. "Press the button." It wasn't until a long time had passed, he later confided, that he realized he had been a witness to a major part of the cover-up operation.

Records were being destroyed all over Washington. The Finance Committee was the only major Nixon affiliate where there was no rush to the shredder. Most of its shredding had been done prior to April 7.

John Dean first heard about the break-in on his way back from Manila on June 18. He had been planning to rest up in San Francisco, but a call to Washington convinced him he must catch the next plane out. On his way home he recalled the meetings in Mitchell's office with Magruder and Liddy. He recalled seeing Liddy flip his charts and talk about "mugging, kidnapping and even a prostitution squad." He claimed to have been shocked, and recalled, after the second meeting, going to Haldeman and saying, "This incredible stuff shouldn't even be discussed in the Attorney General's office."

As Dean's plane floated down to a landing in Washington, he therefore thought of himself as a man with a clear conscience. He had been working in John Ehrlichman's old job as White House counsel only since Ehrlichman had been promoted to head of the Domestic Council. "There was a fantastic title," he said after he had been forced to resign on April 30, 1973. "But I had no real weight. I was counsel to the President, but I didn't counsel the President."

During most of the twenty-seven months he had been in the White House he had seen the President only ten times, never alone. He remembered thinking when a White House job had been offered, "I'm too young."

On setting foot in Washington he began to age. The newspapers at the airport reported the first reaction to the Associated Press discovery that McCord was working for the Committee for the Re-election of the President. John Mitchell, Dean read, was indignant about the story. "McCord is the proprietor of a private security agency who was employed by our committee months ago to assist with the installation of our security system. He has, as we understand it, a number of business clients and interests and we have no knowledge of those relationships. We want to emphasize that this man and the other people involved were not operating either on our behalf or with our consent. I am surprised and dismayed by these reports."

Mitchell, contrary to his protests, knew McCord well enough to place him in charge of security for his family. They had spoken to each other and according to McCord, Mitchell called him "Jim . . . prior to June 17, 1972." McCord had been an employee of the CRP for six months at the time of Mitchell's first attempt to obscure their relationship.

When he reached the White House Dean found the place in pandemonium. Gordon Strachan told him Haldeman had ordered the destruction of wiretap logs in his files, and he had dutifully complied.

The White House attempt to cover up its connection to the crime became intense. The election was at stake. On June 19 Ron Ziegler, in the first of many slashing denials, told a press conference, "I am not going to comment from the White House on a third-rate burglary attempt."

The White House, he implied, was too busy to notice such things; furthermore, he warned darkly, "certain elements may try to stretch this beyond what it is."

What it was and what it was about to become were two different things. The police had found Howard Hunt's name and telephone number in address books taken from two of the arrested men. Next to his name one of them had written, "(W-house)." Despite Ziegler's denial, a White House role in the burglary was beginning to be suspected.

Dean quickly joined in the orgy of criminal complicity taking place around him. The next day Hunt's office safe in the Executive Office Building was broken open at Ehrlichman's direction and its contents were brought to Dean. He was already so completely part of the cover-up that within a few days he was attempting to convince L. Patrick Gray to submit FBI reports on Watergate to him. Dean was not held back for a moment by the thought that these reports were building up evidence which might implicate those for whom Dean was working.

Dean's unethical request was prompted by White House concern over the Mexican money found on Barker. The hundred-dollar bills were numbered consecutively, and the FBI was in the process of routinely tracing them back to the Miami bank in which the original deposit had been made.

The unreported Mexican money was causing so much consternation in the White House that desperate measures were decided on. On June 23 General Vernon Walters, deputy director of the CIA and Richard Helms, CIA director, were summoned to the White House. At 1 P.M. they met with Haldeman and Ehrlichman in Ehrlichman's office.

The message was simple. The Watergate affair might explode into a major political scandal, which might be "exploited" by the political opposition. In order to avoid that terrible threat to national security, Walters should go to Patrick Gray and tell him if the FBI pursued an investigation of Mexican money connected to the Watergate case, the inquiry would compromise CIA activities in Mexico.

Helms was left out of the grimy business, but apparently raised no objection to the request that his deputy dirty his hands.

So conditioned was the general to obeying orders that within an hour, and without any attempt to find out whether the CIA's Mexican operations *would* be compromised by the FBI investigation, he went to Gray's office. Gray, like Walters, new in his office, responded to the general's request for suppression of the investigation by saying he knew the FBI and CIA did not uncover each others operations.

Walters then returned to his office and quickly discovered that what he had been told by Haldeman and Ehrlichman was false. There was no connection between the Watergate money and the CIA's clandestine operations in Mexico.

On June 26 Dean contacted him. He said that he had been authorized to follow up on the discussion he had had with Haldeman and Ehrlichman. After confirming the authorization with Ehrlichman, Walters went to Dean's office. Walters told Dean he had checked out the story and found no CIA involvement. On that inconclusive note he left.

The White House staff apparently felt the FBI and CIA could eventually be brought into line. Of more concern to those trying to protect Nixon was the possibility that the seven members of the burglary team might start to talk. One of the pressures on the burglars was that they were no longer earning a living. All seven of them had to be provided with money. But how could that be done?

These men were accused of a crime. If they were paid openly by the reelection committee, some official notation would have to be made of the expenditure of campaign funds. But such an expenditure could never be justified to the General Accounting Office. Even if it could be, it would be impossible to justify it to the voters if word of it should ever come out.

The alternatives were all unpleasant, the possibility of further compromising the White House was great, yet something had to be done. Since secrecy was imperative, the decision was to turn once again to the CIA.

On June 27 Dean called General Walters and arranged to come to his office. Once there the humorless Dean told Walters some Watergate witnesses "were getting scared and were wobbling." He then asked if there was some way the CIA could post bail and pay the salaries of the accused men as long as they were in jail.

General Walters told the Senate Armed Services Committee that he advised Dean there was no way this could be done. If CIA funds were spent in that way it would implicate the agency in the Watergate crime. Sooner than do that, Walters informed him, he would *resign*. Strange that in the face of a conflict between an order and his conscience, Soldier Walters should have thought of something almost none of the others involved in this intrigue could bring themselves to consider.

The next day Dean was inordinately busy. Still concerned about how the arrested men might be paid he called Walters to the White House and asked him whether he had any ideas. Walters answer was simple, but inadequate for Dean's purposes. Yes, he said, he did have an idea. Anyone who was responsible should be fired.

The problem was beyond Dean's ability to solve. His superiors would have to find the solution.

Dean now turned to other Watergate complications. He approached an agency with which he had been having more success, the FBI. He and Ehrlichman called in Gray and handed Hoover's successor the contents of Hunt's safe, with instructions that the files "should never see the light of day."

Gray was torn by what was going on, yet he wanted to become permanent director, and the only way for that to happen was for President Nixon to send his nomination to the Senate, something Nixon did not do until well into the next year.

Trying to please, Gray called General Walters on

July 5. He referred to his previous conversation with him and pointed out he could not stop the FBI investigation unless he got a letter from Walters saying the probing was threatening CIA's operations in Mexico.

Walters went to see Gray and told him there was no danger to the CIA and the agency had no interest in stopping his investigation. The stiff-backed soldier then told Gray of his alternative to surrender. He informed him that any threat to force him to compromise the CIA would bring about his resignation.

Perhaps that stirred Gray's conscience. That same day he spoke to Clark MacGregor, who had taken over from John Mitchell at CRP on July 1 when the former Attorney General agreed to his wife's wishes to get out of the "dirty business" he was in. Gray told MacGregor he was disturbed at the way Ehrlichman was interfering with the Watergate investigation and he would like to get word to the President.

The next day Nixon called Gray, seemingly on another matter. This conversation, when word of it finally began to emerge eleven months later, proved to be fatal to the cover-up attempt. It revealed the President had direct knowledge of his aides' criminal complicity.

After a while Gray got around to Watergate. He told the President he was confused about the role being played by his aides, and he felt they could cause trouble for him. According to committee investigators, Gray advised his attentive listener: "Mr. President, you are being wounded by men around you, using the FBI and the CIA."

There was a pause on the line and then, Gray reported, the President, avoiding a response, told him to go ahead as he was and ended the conversation.

Prior to this call, the President's only discussions on Watergate were held with Mitchell, Haldeman, and Ehrlichman, all of whom could be depended upon to keep silent, since all of them were deeply involved. Suddenly there was an outsider, someone who had no role in the crime, someone who might at any moment decide to contradict the President when he claimed not to have heard any complaints about his chief aides. It was a breeze out of the dark Arctic night and carried with it a threat to swamp the leaky boat in which these adventurous travellers had embarked.

Still, one could not lose heart. The office of the President was a mighty one. It was possible to blast out denials which, from this seat once occupied by Washington and Lincoln, would drown out the voices of troublemakers.

As the summer wore on, the Watergate case receded from view. McGovern was more interested in the war issue and the newspapers became bored with Larry O'Brien's protests that the Democrats' civil rights and privacy had been violated.

Mitchell, in retirement but not retiring, said this was "another example of sheer demagoguery on the part of Mr. O'Brien."

He then went on to talk to O'Brien's lawyers on September 1, since the Democratic National Chairman was being a bad sport and suing the Republicans for damages. In a pre-trial sworn deposition he incautiously maintained that he had no prior knowledge of the bugging plans. Furthermore, he denied being present at any meeting where bugging was discussed. And he had concluded, "I'll swear to that."

By this time the polls indicated that McGovern was going to lose badly. The White House was elated. All the dirty tricks had paid off and the Nixonettes were hailing the chief with upraised thrusting arms.

Insuring tranquillity was the fact that the seven Watergate thieves were being paid. A solution had been found which did not depend on the CIA. Pay differential ranging from $3,000 down to $1,000 per month, depending on job classification, and legal expenses, were being paid out of Republican campaign contributions. True, the money was coming out of Haldeman's safe and going through Kalmbach's hands on its way to the felons, and in the process serious additional crimes were being committed—but why worry? It almost seemed as if a new category of law had been created; a category which exempted high government officials from certain types of prosecution.

If only the seven would agree to plead guilty, the trial would be a brief formality, and the danger would be passed. The guilty plea would insure that the story would never come out.

And so a new round of crimes was committed as the accused were told they must not cooperate with Judge John J. Sirica. They must remain silent and go to jail for a short while. Their families would be taken care of. Executive clemency, which could be granted only by the President, would get them out in no time. Then there would be jobs for all.

It probably would have worked. Five of them pleaded guilty soon after their trial began on January 8, 1973. The other two, McCord and Liddy, defended themselves without revealing who had inspired their entry or what they intended to do with their information.

McCord was the only one causing trouble. He was privately telling the conspirators he would not remain silent much longer.

John Dean, dangerously widening the conspiratorial circle, instructed John Caulfield, former New York City policeman, who had been a White House aide, to contact the former CIA agent and offer him executive clemency. McCord had gotten his job with the CRP on Caulfield's recommendation, and they were friends.

In a scene which could only have been contrived by a former CIA agent and a former cop, the two rendezvoused at the side of the Potomac, within sight of the great monuments of the Capitol. During their "friendly" discussion, Caulfield chided McCord for being the only defendant not going along with "the game plan." He told him that he had been authorized "from way up at the top" to tell him he would get executive clemency. When later asked by the Ervin Committee what John Dean's words conveyed to him, Caulfield said he assumed the authorization had come from the President.

McCord would not yield. He objected to the idea that Magruder and others involved in the plot were being protected, but he was going to have to go to jail. "Some people are more equal than others," he remarked bitterly.

On January 30, 1973, all rational reasons to worry seemed to have disappeared. Liddy and McCord were found guilty and remained silent. Judge Sirica accused the Justice Department prosecutors of not asking probing questions and not trying to find out who else had been involved in the planning of the burglary. However, that was a minor affront.

The important thing was that Watergate was now an episode which, eventually, would interest only the most nit-picking historians. Republicans could rejoice that Nixon confidant Pat Buchanan's description of the break-in was the one most people would remember: it was merely "a few Cubans reading Larry O'Brien's mail."

CHAPTER XIV

## Nixon's Guilt

"All the power in the White House," H. R. Haldeman explained just prior to the Watergate exposures, "is in one man. I don't think there are seconds or thirds or fourths."

This was testimony from an authoritative source. Haldeman was explaining that no matter how powerful he appeared to the uninitiated, there was only one person who made the decisions.

At the same time, although many details about the wiretapping, burglary, espionage, financial manipulations, sabotage and covert use of the FBI and CIA, both before and after Watergate break-in, are still unknown, one fact has been clearly established. Dozens of men took part in this far flung series of conspiracies, but only one man could reasonably be expected to benefit from all of them.

The motive behind all of these crimes is identical. When stripped of the rationalizations supplied by apprehended felons, the driving force behind each obscenity was to perpetuate Richard Nixon in office.

No doubt some of the minor figures who actually did the breaking-and-entering, the dreary work of monitoring at lonely stations, the sleezy work of distortion and deceit, had different dreams. Some, like Bernard Barker, might have thought they were taking part in the first stage of a new Bay of Pigs operation. Others might have felt if they stayed close to the action some crumbs might drop off the banquet table.

But whatever the supplementary motives, they all knew that the man "on the highest level," operating through his underlings, wanted the dirty work done. Most of them had not met him, but their concept of the

151

public man was not violated by suggestions of surreptitious, double-dealing, criminal behavior proposed in his name.

For many months there was a question as to whether he knew what was going on. Republican Senator Edward W. Brooke, of Massachusetts, did not share those doubts about the leader of his party. He told "Meet The Press" interviewers:

"It is difficult to understand how persons working with the President would not make known to him an enterprise of this magnitude involving hundreds of thousands of dollars and involving such a potential risk.

"It is inconceivable to me that they would not have told the President about this matter. In fact, that they wouldn't have asked for his approval or disapproval."

The illumination shed on this point by Senator Brooke and H. R. Haldeman is no longer necessary. The President has conceded that he knew most, if not all, except in minor detail. That concession has emerged slowly, and then only as it became clear that a cunningly phrased confession, with obfuscating explanations, had to be made just before an accusation was proved.

At first he compounded his guilt by denying all and removing himself from the scene. At a White House press conference on June 22, six days after the break-in, and after accusations of White House complicity in the break-in had been circulating for six days, the President prepared to listen to the first question on the subject.

"Mr. O'Brien has said that the people who bugged his headquarters had a direct link to the White House. Have you had any sort of investigation made to determine whether this is true?"

A humble reporter, representing a much maligned press, had instantly pointed out the only logical and responsible line of action for the President. Serious accusations had been made. The only course open was to investigate. Had that investigation taken place?

The President: "Mr. Ziegler and also Mr. Mitchell, speaking for the campaign committee, have responded to questions on this in great detail."

This was not true. Mitchell had issued a denial but gone into *no* detail. Ziegler had called it a "third-rate burglary" lying outside the political process, but refused to comment beyond that attempt to make the matter somewhat comical.

The President continued: "They have stated my position and have also stated the facts accurately."

There is a suggestion here that he had conducted an investigation, since there was no other way to ascertain that the facts were accurate without such an investigation. He reinforced that impression, without quite saying it, in his next comment.

"This kind of activity, as Mr. Ziegler has indicated, has no place whatever in our electoral process, or in our governmental process. And, as Mr. Ziegler has stated, the White House has had no involvement whatever in this *particular* incident. [Italics added]"

The President was saying that he was against this type of activity, not only in politics, but burglary as part of "our governmental process" was also against his principles. However, as is his wont, the next sentence contained a hint that there were other incidents, aside from this "particular" one in which the White House might have been involved. Again a fact which could only be substantiated by an investigation.

He then concluded, "As far as the matter now is concerned, it is under investigation, as it should be, by the proper legal authorities, by the District of Columbia police and by the FBI. I will not comment on these matters, particularly since possible criminal charges are involved."

But the reporter had wanted to know whether *he* was investigating. Everyone knew the police were investigating. They had a gang of burglars in jail. An investigation was automatic. Since large amounts of suspicious money were found on men interfering with a Federal election, it was obvious the FBI was investigating. But had he called in Haldeman and Ehrlichman and told them to investigate? Had he sat down with John Mitchell, whom he was seeing every day on matters concerning the campaign, and asked him who this CRP employee McCord was and what he was doing in the Democratic National Committee offices in the middle of the night?

Even more important, he knew Howard Hunt had been on the White House staff—in fact, had an office on the third floor. On that very day the FBI was questioning John Dean in a nearby office as to whether Hunt had worked in the White House, and Dean, who had poured over the contents of Hunt's safe two days earlier, lied that he did not know. Had the President raised any question about Hunt's connection to the crime? Liddy had also been at the White House. He was a key figure with the Finance Committee. Had he tried to find out how Liddy could have become involved in such a thing?

There was no indication that the President was asking any of those questions. There were two obvious conclusions to draw. Either he was asking them and getting answers he did not like and, therefore, was determined to say nothing and participate in a cover-up; or he was not asking those questions because he already knew their answers and was determined no one else should.

There was, of course, the possibility that he was concerned about some aspect of national security. He knew Liddy and Hunt were part of the so-called "Plumbers" unit he had ordered set up on the previous summer in the White House. If he admitted knowing them at that June 22 press conference, then he would strip the cloak of secrecy from the covert things he had authorized them to do.

His position was untenable. The slightest admission would reveal him as a ruthless man willing to use any technique to destroy his opposition and maintain himself in power. For although an agile mind, freed of ethical restraints normally accepted by citizens living in a democracy, might invent some semi-plausible excuse for pursuing Daniel Ellsberg to the shelter of his psychiatrist's couch, it was unlikely that a shadow of the same plausibility could be found for reading Larry O'Brien's mail.

Silence was the only refuge.

It was not until August 29 that he was once again provoked into a comment on Watergate. Three days earlier the General Accounting Office had revealed "apparent violations" of the new election law concerning the $350,000 in Stans' safe. The GAO report stated $114,000 of Stans' money had ended up in Barker's Miami account. Banner headlines on the subject reawakened interest in the crime.

On August 29 the President informed his press conference that John Dean, his counsel, had been conducting an investigation into the case. He indicated Dean had given him a report absolving everyone close to his heart.

"I can say categorically that his [Dean's] investigation indicates that no one in the White House staff, no one in this administration, presently employed, was involved in this very bizarre incident."

There were two major problems with this statement. It was not true that Dean was then, or ever had been, conducting an investigation. He had scarcely seen the President since June 17, much less had a conference at which he was directed to conduct an investigation.

Dean told *Newsweek* Magazine months later of his reaction: "Here was the President of the United States reassuring the American people on the basis of a report that didn't exist."

After the ax had fallen, Dean commented about his sudden sense of unease on hearing his name bandied around in such cavanter manner. "I was locked in concrete on national television on August 29," he said remorsefully.

Nixon was depending on Dean's inability to publicly confound his statement. And as long as Dean did not summon up the courage to contradict him, he had found a witness to support his image of vigilance and innocence.

The second problem was his use of the modifying phrase "presently employed" when insisting that no one working on the White House staff was involved. Although it eventually developed even that was not true (Haldeman, Ehrlichman, Colson, and Dean were still at their desks), it suggested that some culprits had been "formerly employed." Liddy and Hunt fell into that category, as did John Mitchell.

The only inference to draw from the warning flag he had hoisted in the midst of his denial was that he was aware, although he insisted he was not, that there had been White House complicity with "this very bizarre incident."

He then concluded with an outstanding example of the preacher who was unable to practice what he preached.

"What really hurts in matters of this sort is not the fact that they occur, because overzealous people in campaigns do things that are wrong. What really hurts is if you try to cover it up."

In the very process of covering up, he was moralizing about the harmful nature of the process.

For the next few weeks, all questions about Watergate were answered with references to the President's August 29 assurance that John Dean's investigation had cleared everybody. Reporters who attempted to get Ron Ziegler to reveal whether Dean had discovered who had ordered the bugging or why it was ordered were told to read the President's statement.

On September 15 the seven man burglary team was indicted by the grand jury under the guidance of the Justice Department's prosecutors. John Dean claims there was rejoicing in the White House. Other indictments have been expected specifically. At this point, Dean says, Bob Haldeman took him into the President's office, where a happy Nixon supposedly told him, "Good job, John. Bob told me what a great job you've done."

For the next three weeks everything seemed to be under control. *Editor & Publisher* reported 668 papers backed Nixon, only 38 endorsed McGovern. The outcome of the election no longer seemed in doubt. As a mark of his confidence, Nixon scheduled a rare press conference. The first question must have made him regret his rashness. "Mr. President, what are you planning to do to defend yourself against the charges of corruption in your administration?"

Almost casually he elaborated on the implicit accusation in the reporters question: "Well, I have noted such charges; as a matter of fact, I have noted that this administration has been charged with being the most corrupt in history, and I have been charged with being the most deceitful President in history."

A few minutes later a reporter, provoked by four months of frustration over his inability to get a straight answer on Watergate, got off one of the most sharply worded questions ever aimed at a President.

"Mr. President, don't you think that your administration and the public would be served considerably and that the men under indictment would be treated better, if *you* people would come through and make a clean breast about what *you* were trying to get done at the Watergate?"

The President of the United States was being accused before the world of taking part in a burglary. All he could do was make believe he had not heard the accusation.

"One thing that has always puzzled me about it is why anybody would have tried to get anything out of the Watergate. Be that as it may that decision having been made at a lower level, with which I had no knowledge, and, as I have pointed out—"

The President was admitting the decision to burglarize Democratic Headquarters had been "made at a lower level" by people in his official family, yet months had passed and he was still maintaining the fictitious "Dean Report" position that everyone around him was cleared.

The argumentative reporter was astounded. Running out of patience, he broke into what the President was saying. "Surely you know now, sir."

"I certainly feel that under the circumstances that we have to look at what has happened and to put the matter into perspective," he said.

There was a fleeting thought that the truth was about

to emerge. Perhaps the President was about to speak about *national security* considerations that had driven the Republicans to the point where selfless thoughts of country had made them desperate enough to commit a criminal act against the Democrats. Whatever his reasons for not speaking out, the President abruptly changed the topic of conversation, using the FBI to cover his tracks.

"Now when we talk about a clean breast, let's look at what has happened. The FBI has assigned 133 agents to this investigation. It followed out 1,800 leads. It conducted 1,500 interviews."

Here was a revelation that the President was not merely depending on the Dean Report. He knew the exact statistics on FBI investigations—investigations which, at this point, had largely uncovered the dimensions of the Republican effort to interfere with the honest conduct of the Presidential election. It is unreasonable to assume that, knowing this much, he did not know all. Yet he maintained as late as April 30, 1973, that he had known nothing, and had trusted in the assurances given by his loyal subordinates.

But what he said at this press conference made that later assertion appear deceitful. "I agree with the amount of effort that was put into it [by the FBI]. I wanted every lead carried out to the end because I wanted to be sure that no member of the White House staff and no man or woman in a position of major responsibility in the Committee for Re-election had anything to do with this kind of reprehensible activity."

Having "wanted to be sure" no member of his staff was involved, he was apparently now maintaining that he was sure. No heads were rolling. And then in a successful endeavor to cut off any further questions, he said, with barely suppressed cynicism:

"I am going to follow the good advice, which I appreciate, of the members of the press corps, my constant, and I trust will always continue to be, very responsible critics.

"I stepped into one on that when you recall I made

inadvertently a comment in Denver about an individual who had been indicted in California, the Manson case. I was vigorously criticized for making any comment about the case, so of course, I know you would want me to follow the same single standard by not commenting on this case."

The lid was on. No more comment before election. People were not getting excited about Watergate. Many of them were so intent on rejecting McGovern's candidacy they did not want to consider the possibility that the only other man they were going to have a chance to vote for had set into motion events which led to criminal acts.

Until October 10 it was possible to downgrade the importance of the Watergate break-in. Until that date it seemed like an isolated event. The plans of the same men to burglarize McGovern campaign headquarters as soon as the job was done at the Watergate were not known. Neither was the incredible amount of espionage and sabotage committed by Nixon's men yet common knowledge. Aside from some scandals associated with the financial manipulations of Stans' Committee, the only illegality seemed to involve seven men who grubbed around in Larry O'Brien's office.

On October 10 the *Washington Post*'s indefatigable team, Carl Bernstein, twenty-nine, and Bob Woodward, thirty, widened the significance of the accusations. They revealed the existence of a network of agents directed by White House and CRP officials who were involved in a massive political espionage conspiracy. A few days later they named Donald Segretti as the major Republican saboteur and revealed he took his orders from the President's appointment secretary, Dwight Chapin. By October 25 the two *Post* reporters, well on their way to a thoroughly deserved Pulitzer Prize, exposed Haldeman's secret campaign fund and said the sabotage was being paid for by him.

The President let his thirty second spot commercials do his talking, and none of them were about Watergate. Jeb Magruder, who revealed on May 25, 1973, that he

was going to plead guilty for his role in the Watergate
conspiracies and tell what he knew of the complicity of
other White House officials, was one of the few who was
willing to speak out at that time.

"When this is over," Haldeman's confidant said,
"you'll know that there were only seven people who
knew about Watergate, and they are the seven indicted
by the grand jury."

Ziegler added that no one presently employed in the
White House had "directed activities of sabotage, spying
or espionage. . . . If anyone had been involved in any
such activity, they would no longer be at the White
House because this is activity that we do not condone
and do not tolerate."

How much credence could be put in White House
denials became clear months later when the President
confessed that he had personally condoned spying and
espionage, and had been doing so since 1969.

However, the finesse worked. Nixon won by a landslide, next to Lyndon Johnson's winning margin the
largest majority in history. Interest in Watergate again
diminished. The death of Dorothy Hunt, wife of the
Watergate coordinator, in a plane crash on December 8,
was scarcely noticed. Howard Hunt explained the $10,-
000 in hundred-dollar bills found in his wife's purse as
merely some cash she was planning to invest in Chicago
real estate. The fact that she was the reluctant conduit
for payoffs to the apprehended felons did not come to
light for months.

When Dwight Chapin resigned on January 29 to become the director of market planning for United Air
Lines, just as the guilty verdicts were about to be handed
down against the Watergate Seven, it looked as if the
last tidying strokes were being delivered on a successful
cover-up.

However, the Senate was not going along in a fashion
completely to the President's pleasure. There was re-
vived talk of hearings, to be chaired by the prestigious
Constitutionalist Sam Ervin, Democrat of North Caro-
lina. In an endeavor to discourage this mortal threat to

the elaborate structure of concealment, the President let it be known that "executive privilege" would keep any of his staff members from testifying.

On January 31 the President outlined his views on this subject in a press conference. The stalwart CBS reporter Dan Rather, called it Nixon's worst confrontation with the press since his "you won't have Nixon to kick around" conference in 1962. Rather described him as being nervous from the start, his voice weak, his body tense, and his temper quick.

After snapping that he would never forgive those who had been unwilling to fight in Vietnam until they paid the price, he indicated what he considered the price anyone breaking a law must pay. "The price is a criminal penalty for disobeying the laws of the United States."

Within a short time he was embroiled in a controversy over what appeared to be a new extension of executive privilege. Formerly Presidents had maintained that conversations between themselves and people working for them were privileged, and such persons could not be forced to divulge what had been said. As a Congressman in 1948, Nixon had objected to even this limited definition which was then being expressed by President Truman.

But under the pressure of the Senatorial investigation which he could see looming on the horizon, he made a dramatic extension of the censorship powers inherent in this doctrine. If *any* individual was called before a Congressional committee on wrongdoing, it would have to *then* be decided whether he would refuse to testify on the grounds of executive privilege. And the criteria would not be whether he was being asked to reveal conversations with the President. The decision would have to be made on each case. How was the decision to be reached?

"He will come down here [the accused government official] and Mr. Dean, the White House counsel, will then advise him as to whether or not we approve it."

Under close questioning he retreated somewhat, saying he was "not going to use executive privilege as a

shield for conversations that might be just embarrassing
to us . . ."

It is interesting to note at this point that most Americans were reluctant to believe Nixon had anything to
do with the scandals involving his administration. The
polls recorded over 60 per cent of those sampled
thought he was doing a fine job.

March, 1973, was the month in which it became obvious that the labored effort of the Nixon Administration
to conceal its involvement in a wide variety of crimes
was not going to work. It was a month of crisis for
Richard Nixon, a crisis of his own making.

At a March 2 press conference he was asked to comment on the case, now that it was over. Oh, but it
wasn't, the President corrected. It would not be proper
for him to comment while the convicted men were
appealing the verdict.

Then, ignoring his resolve, he immediately launched
into another effort to still the barking dogs of the press.

"I will simply say with regard to the Watergate case
what I have said previously that the investigation conducted by Mr. Dean, the White House counsel, in
which, incidentally, he had access to the FBI records on
this particular matter because I directed him to conduct
this investigation, indicates that no one on the White
House staff, at the time he conducted the investigation
—that was last July and August—was involved or had
knowledge of the Watergate matter and, as far as the
balance of the case is concerned, it is now under investigation by a Congressional committee and that committee should go forward, conduct its investigation in an
even-handed way, going into charges made against both
candidates, both political parties . . ."

The last was to become a major theme in his final
defense. All politicians did things they were not proud
of at one time or another. Why should the Republicans
be singled out just because they happened to be caught?

It was a particularly myopic defense, since no one
was accusing Nixon's men of minor indiscretions, and

no one was accusing the Democrats of major criminal activity.

But, a reporter pointed out, the committee which was presently trying to make up its mind whether to confirm L. Patrick Gray, whose nomination as permanent FBI director Nixon had finally sent to the Senate, was suggesting that this very John Dean, in whom the President placed so much faith, might be called to testify on the Watergate case. At the same time they might want to question Dean about the strange relationship between the FBI and the White House, which Gray's inadvertently frank testimony was bringing to light. "Would you object to that?"

"Of course!" the President shot back.

And then the simplest question of all from that group of suspicious men. "Why?"

"Well," the President began, clearly embarrassed, ". . . because it is executive privilege. I mean you can't —I, of course—no President could ever agree to allow the counsel to the President to go down and testify before a committee."

Determined not to be put off so easily, another reporter, ignoring the fact that the signal had been given that the conference was over, shot out, "If the counsel was involved in an illegal or improper act and the *prima facie* case came to light, then would you change the rules relative to the White House counsel?"

He was being asked, in effect, whether he would be willing to let his counsel avoid prosecution, when there was substantial evidence of his guilt, by hiding behind the door of the Oval Office. The answer should have been a straightforward *no,* since he had stated many times he did not believe any man should be beyond the law.

Instead he equivocated: "I do not expect that to happen and if it should happen I would have to answer that question at that point."

Dean had once again seen his name used to sanction the cover-up. In pushing him out in front of the pack the President was making him an obvious target. He was beginning to draw fire.

But this was the way the President fought. Each man was there to serve his purposes. Wasn't that, after all, how each of them should be proud to be used?

At about this time he told Saul Pett of Associated Press, in an exclusive interview, "I believe in the battle, whether it's the battle of a campaign or the battle of this office, which is a continuing battle. It's always there, wherever you go. I, perhaps, carry it more than others because that's my way."

It was a pugnacious view of life, phrased in military terms. It brought a response from Senator Muskie, who was still smarting from the pernicious treatment given him the previous year by Nixon's saboteurs. He predicted Nixon's leadership would someday be rejected as "negative and narrow."

By the middle of March, that day did not seem too far off. In an effort to hold back the flood of information now threatening to burst forth, the President announced he was extending executive privilege to past, as well as present members of the White House staff.

At his March 15 press conference he angrily stated that even if it meant the defeat of Gray's nomination, he would not allow John Dean to be questioned—even "informally"—by the Senate committee.

It was clear by this time Gray was going to be sacrificed. For some reason that Richard Nixon knew, but that the rest of his countrymen could only guess at, he did not want John Dean's mind probed by Congressional investigators. He was, no doubt, angry at the concessions Gray had made to honesty in his prolonged cross-examination. During the course of the hearings he revealed that the FBI had, early on, discovered that the President's personal attorney, Herbert Kalmbach, had been involved with Dwight Chapin in hiring chief saboteur Donald Segretti, and paying him $40,000.

Most respectfully a reporter asked: "Can you tell us, sir, did you know of that relationship, and did you know of that transaction, and if not, can you tell us your opinion of it now that it has been revealed by Mr. Gray."

There were three possible answers. Yes, I knew. No, I did not know. And the third answer, which he gave: "This gives me an opportunity to not only answer that question, but many others that I note you have been asking Mr. Ziegler." After three hundred more muddied words it boiled down to *no comment*.

However, before he turned away from Watergate, he wanted it understood, "I have confidence in all of the White House people who have been named. I will express that confidence again."

Richard Nixon is not a man to go down with the ship. It was probable, at this point, he still felt there was a good chance he could squeeze by. What was not clear was that the President had held his last press conference for some time to come. The events which were about to burst on him made it inconceivable he would again expose himself to even the most limited type of questioning from the press.

John Dean says that on March 20 he finally got to see the President. He claims to have warned him that the scandal was much more widespread than he had earlier believed. He insists that he told him there was a "cancer" in his administration that had to be cut out.

However, the most important single event since the burglars had been apprehended had already been set in motion, and, although he did not realize it, control of the situation was no longer in the President's hands.

On March 19 James McCord wrote a remarkable letter in his jail cell, which he mailed to Judge Sirica, without first showing it to his lawyer. On March 23, as he was about to announce sentence on the convicted Watergate burglars, the judge suddenly produced McCord's letter and read it to the open court. The impeachment of Richard Nixon was from this moment on a matter which could not lightly be brushed aside.

In the letter McCord charged that "there was political pressure applied to the defendants to plead guilty and remain silent." Not merely pressure, but *political* pressure. With the testimony of John Caulfield on May 23, it became obvious that the pressure had come from highest levels of the White House.

McCord wrote that "perjury occurred during the trial in matters highly material to the very structure, orientation and impact of the Government's case." He was shortly to testify that it was Magruder who had perjured himself.

His final claim was that there was a plot to obstruct justice. "Others involved in the Watergate operation were not identified during the trial, when they could have been by those testifying."

He told the judge that "members of my family have expressed fear for my life if I disclose knowledge of the facts in this matter." However, he wanted to speak privately to the judge and provide more details. He said he did not "feel confident in talking with an FBI agent, in testifying before a grand jury whose U.S. attorneys work for the Department of Justice, or with other Government representatives."

The top was blown off the case. There was no way to imagine that the truth could continue to be concealed.

The next day, as more and more names of men close to President Nixon were being mentioned as participants in the Watergate crimes, Senate Republican leader Hugh Scott came out of the White House and said the President had told him: "I have nothing to hide. The White House has nothing to hide. I repeat, we have nothing to hide and you are authorized to make that statement in my name."

From this point on admission after startling admission was made by the President. It is clear he had used Scott poorly, but not clear that the leader of the Senate Republicans felt poorly used.

That same day McCord told Senator Ervin's investigators that John Dean and Jeb Magruder knew about the bugging in advance. The walls were closing in on these two—and, with them, on Richard Nixon.

Even loyal Republicans were turning on him. Senator Lowell P. Weicker, one of the three Republican

members of the Ervin Committee which was soon to be
exploring all aspects of the story on nationwide television, let his anger show on March 26. He told reporters
specific violation of the law "is not the only issue involved, although some people in the administration
would like to have it drawn that way, as narrowly as
possible. It's just as bad in my book for certain persons
at the Presidential level to condone illegal practices. . . .
I don't give a damn if there's a law on the books against
it or not."

"Does the Watergate lead directly to the President?"
he was asked. After some hesitation he said, "Somebody
had to start it. Somebody had to abet it. Mr. Hunt and
Mr. Liddy and Mr. McCord, et al., didn't just get together in a barroom one night and decide they were
going to do something gratuitous for the Republican
Party."

By late March the President's judgment was betraying
him into new and more serious crimes. The story did
not emerge until May 22, when Elliot Richardson was
before a Senate Committee seeking confirmation of his
nomination as Nixon's third Attorney General in little
more than a year. Kleindienst had finally felt compelled
to resign on April 30 because too many of his "personal
friends" were being prosecuted by his Justice Department.

Richardson told the committee he had been contacted by Ehrlichman on April 30 and asked to advise
Egil Krogh on a matter of some importance. At their
luncheon, Richardson informed the Senators, Krogh
told him of his role in the burglary of Dr. Fielding's
office in the summer of 1971.

He also informed him that he had told the President
about it "in late March." An amazing statement. Krogh
had informed the President of a crime. The law was
precise. When a citizen hears of a crime, he must report
it to the police. Most ordinary law abiding citizens know
that. Certainly a member of the bar, such as the President, was aware of his duty.

He had indicated on June 22, 1972, five days after

the Watergate break-in, what his attitude was on the subject of obedience to the law.

"When we talk about the spirit of the law and the letter of the law, my evaluation is that it is the responsibility of all, a high moral responsibility to obey the law and to obey it totally."

The President was also obligated to inform Judge William Byrne that evidence germaine to the Ellsberg trial, then in session in Los Angeles, had been brought to his attention.

Instead the President allowed himself to become an instrument in the obstruction of justice. Not only did he refrain from communicating his knowledge to the judge, he now entered a conspiracy which tainted the conduct of the trial.

On April 5, approximately two weeks after Krogh had spoken to him, he had John Ehrlichman contact Judge Byrne and ask him to come to San Clemente. That day the President had withdrawn L. Patrick Gray's nomination from consideration by the Senate. It had become clear that Gray would never be confirmed. The Senate had become painfully aware of the political manner in which he had run his sensitive office, and the ease with which he had succumbed to every pressure Richard Nixon placed on him.

Ehrlichman came straight to the point. Would the judge like to become the director of the FBI? While his head was still spinning the President came upon them and shook his hand warmly, letting him know how proud he was to meet such a fine man.

The judge seemed to have sensed some impropriety. He averred that it would be impossible for him to accept the job while the case was still on. However, his sense of unease did not keep him from a second meeting with Ehrlichman two days later in Santa Monica.

Another two weeks passed before the President allowed Assistant Attorney General Petersen and several other advisors to pressure him into obeying the law.

What he had done, in effect, was to attempt to bribe a judge. Ehrlichman, who knew from Krogh and the

*Nixon's Guilt* 169

President that his role in the Fielding burglary was about
to be exposed, was offering a choice position to the man
who was about to receive that information. There has
never been a similar case of bribery in the history of
this country. There has never been an instant in which
a presiding judge has been summoned by the President
and offered a promotion while the judge has been in the
process of determining the destiny of that President's
administration. A mistrial was only the first measure
that had to be taken to right the imbalance of justice
caused by this gross attempt to subvert the judicial
system.

On April 5 John Dean went to the Justice Department's prosecutors to talk about Watergate, and the
alibis began to come apart. Robert Reisner, Magruder's
assistant, told the grand jury on April 11 that Magruder
received the transcripts of the bugged Watergate conversations. Reisner later told the Ervin Committee he
sent a duplicate to John Mitchell.

On April 14 Jeb Magruder went to Assistant U.S.
Attorney Earl Silbert and, after an abortive attempt to
negotiate immunity in exchange for what he knew of the
involvement of White House figures, dictated an affidavit. In it he implicated Mitchell and Dean in the original planning of the burglary and bugging; he also
accused them of pressuring him to perjure himself at
the Watergate trial and before several sessions of the
grand jury.

The next day Attorney General Kleindienst and his
assistant, Henry Petersen, went to see the President
with the news that a case had been worked up from
many sources which suggested that, at a minimum, his
staff was deeply involved in perjury and obstruction of
justice. From this moment on Dean felt that he was
*persona non grata.*

The President now realized he no longer had a choice.
He was either going to have to expose some of the
seamier aspects of the scandal himself, or others were
going to expose them. The suit brought by Common
Cause against the Re-election Finance Committee's vio-

lations of the campaign laws was moving toward a trial date. Larry O'Brien's suit on behalf of the Democrats would also soon be in the courts. These were not cases being prosecuted by employees of the Justice Department who might be expected to tread gently on any matter affecting their boss. Many things were bound to come out as men like Magruder were brought to the bar and faced with the decision of whether they were willing to pay the penalty for perjury.

On April 17 a somber Nixon suddenly appeared in the White House press room. During the next three minutes, before a startled group of newspaper people, he read the first installment of his confession.

In the first of two brief statements, he immediately surrendered on the issue of executive privilege. "All members of the White House staff will appear voluntarily when requested by the [Ervin] committee. They will testify under oath and they will answer fully all proper questions."

The second statement was the bombshell. "On March 21, as a result of serious charges which came to my attention, some of which were publicly reported, I began intensive new inquiries into this whole matter."

It was instantly apparent the President was going to continue his dissembling about the crimes surrounding Watergate. Did he seriously expect people to believe new charges had to be made in order to cause him to intensively investigate the multitude of allegations which had been surfacing for ten months? What had he been doing since the break-in? Was he so completely isolated in the Quiet Room that not even a whisper of illegality intruded? Surely Gray's telephone warning on July 6 had been enough to alert any man who was not himself so compromised that warnings elicited terror rather than a desire for truth.

"I can report today that there have been major developments in the case concerning which it would be improper to be more specific now, except to say that real progress has been made in finding the truth."

But, he later conceded, at this point he knew the

truth. He was in the process of making up his mind whether Haldeman and Ehrlichman would have to resign. He had already determined John Dean was expendable, and Ziegler was no longer issuing statements indicating the President's full confidence in his counsel.

Then perhaps the purpose of the statement was revealed in his contention that "it would be improper to be more specific now . . ." Wasn't this another way of saying, let's stop talking about the major developments which are appearing daily in the *Washington Post,* the *New York Times,* the *Los Angeles Times,* and weekly in *Time* and *Newsweek* Magazines?

That he did not intend to move too rapidly was revealed in the next paragraph. "If any person in the executive branch or in the Government is indicted by the grand jury, my policy will be to immediately suspend him."

Undoubtedly the impression he wished to convey was one of utter fairness. A man is not guilty until convicted in a court of law. But men who run the government are not weighed on that scale. A White House aide does not have to remain in his job until it is proven that he broke some law and the jail door closes behind him. Presidents have fired men who are suspected of such minor offenses as inefficiency, disloyalty, or not smiling at the proper times. Here was a President who was going to conduct "intensive new inquiries into the whole matter," and then wait for grand jury indictments before he even went as far as to "suspend" the suspected employees.

His intention of obstructing, rather than cooperating with, any endeavor to get at the truth was emphasized when he said:

"I have expressed to the appropriate authorities my view that no individual holding, in the past or at present, a position of major importance in the Administration should be given immunity from prosecution."

In 1969 he had been the leader in a Congressional effort to grant immunity to crime syndicate figures who might be willing to squeal on their boss. He insisted at that time the only way to get at the higher-ups was to let a few of the small fry escape prosecution. Suddenly that principle so vital for the detection of crime lords was no longer valid when it was applied to other lords.

But, he wanted to assure everyone, "I condemn any attempts to cover up in this case, no matter who is involved."

Rejecting any attempt to question him, he fled from the room.

Ziegler then met with the press and informed the incensed newsmen that all the statements of the previous months were "inoperative." In short, the President had previously been lying.

John Dean, feeling the concrete had hardened and he was about to be dumped into the river, issued a public statement two days later which was startling in its implications. Not seeking the mandatory White House clearance for statements and bypassing Ron Ziegler completely, he had his trembling secretary call the news services and inform the world that "some may hope or think that I will become a scapegoat in the Watergate case. Anyone who believes this does not know me, know the true facts, nor understand our system of justice."

How was it possible for anyone around the President to believe that, after this, the truth would not come out? Even if some method were found to soothe Dean, surely they must have realized that some grand jury, some Congressional committee, some engine of impeachment had been fueled by this threatening blast.

Ziegler quickly called together the press corps and said "the process now underway is not one to find scapegoats but one to get at the truth." He would not, however, repeat the President's previous expressions of support for Dean. He said that although still not suspended, Dean was no longer working on any Watergate investigation.

Only the most reckless would now hesitate to take precautions. Informed that they must soon appear before the grand jury, Haldeman and Ehrlichman hired barrister John J. Wilson. Wilson was known as a lawyers's lawyer, and had made a reputation defending many of them against criminal charges.

The President called Wilson to the White House on two separate occasions and spent several hours conferring with him. One presumes he was not seeking personal advice, but was being informed about Wilson's two clients. Still they remained at their desks, although in hindsight it is clear the President was completely aware of their felonious behavior. It was one thing to fire a clerk who knows only what is in the office file, another thing to fire men who knew what was in the President's head.

On Easter Sunday, April 22, the President made an effort to unruffle Dean's feathers. Although he knew Dean was guilty of criminal acts, he phoned him, in what must have been an effort to gain a little time.

Dean shouted out the news. "He said I was still his counsel and wished me and my pretty wife the best and told us to go to church and smile well for everyone."

How did young John react? "I thought it was a stroking move—don't let old John get out of hand."

But *everything* was out of hand. On April 27 John Ehrlichman told FBI investigators that, *acting on Nixon's orders,* he had directed Liddy and Hunt to conduct a "secret" investigation which had resulted in the break-in to the office of Ellsberg's psychiatrist.

On April 30 Richard Nixon made his second confession, one that was much more damaging. It was not as lachrymose as the original Checkers speech in 1952, but then he did not have the dignity of the Presidency to sustain him.

It was 9:00 on a Monday night and he sat at his desk in the Oval Office, a bust of Lincoln to one side, a family picture guarding his other flank. He began by assuring everyone he was speaking "from my heart."

What brought him to this terrible moment was that "charges of illegal activity during and preceding the 1972 Presidential election and charges that responsible officials participated in efforts to cover that illegal activity" had been made against his administration and

officials of his re-election committee. He admitted, "The
inevitable result of these charges has been to raise serious questions about the integrity of the White House
itself."

He narrowed the scope of his denial at this point.
"Last June 17 while I was in Florida trying to get a
few days' rest after my visit to Moscow, I first learned
from news reports of the Watergate break-in."

There was the image here of the Chief Executive
wearied by the exertions of global diplomacy, attempting to recuperate. However, he had not just returned
from Moscow as he was implying. He had returned on
June 2, had been to Key Biscayne to rest, had returned
to his duties at the White House and was once again
back in the Florida sun on June 16.

He specifically refrained from saying that he did not
have knowledge his team of "Plumbers" were going to
someday try to bug Democratic headquarters. He re-
stricted himself to the assertion that he had "first learned
from news reports of the Watergate break-in."

For the first time he revealed what his reaction had
been. "I was appalled at this senseless, illegal action,
and I was shocked to learn that employees of the re-election committee were apparently among those guilty."

So here at last was his acknowledgment that he had
known from the first that employees of the re-election
committee, Liddy and Hunt, who were, more impor-
tantly, former White House aides, had been involved in
the Watergate break-in. Then he had lied on June 22
when he had said "the White House has had no involvement whatever in this particular incident."

At this point he began the process of shifting the
burden of guilt to his subordinates. "As the investigation
went forward," he said earnestly, "I repeatedly asked
those conducting the investigation whether there was
any reason to believe that members of my administration were in any way involved." It was only their "repeated assurances" that kept him in the dark.

"I believed the reports I was getting, because I had
faith in the persons from whom I was getting them . . ."

It was now clear he was not only getting them from evil John Dean, but from "persons." But, he was informing the nation, they were all just as bad. They had all deceived him.

Then he blundered. "Until March of this year, I remained convinced that the denials were true and that the charges of involvement by members of the White House staff were false."

He had opened himself to serious charges of malfeasance. The head of the FBI had warned him on July 6, 1972 that the men around him were "mortally wounding" him. How had it been possible for him to depend upon them for information from that moment on? Was this not an indication that rather than informants, they were his confederates?

In a show of innocence that was blinding he continued to lacerate his "friends." In March information had come to him that "there was a real possibility that some of these charges were true and suggesting further that there had been an effort to conceal the facts both from the public—from you—and from me."

Therefore he had taken over the investigation personally, something the citizenry might have expected he would have done on June 17. No longer was he going to depend on those rascals who had been withholding information from their trusting President.

"At the same time," he explained, "I was determined not to take precipitive action and to avoid if at all possible any action that would appear to reflect on innocent people."

He does not seem to be quite the avenging angel here. Nor does he appear to be the Richard Nixon with whom everyone was familiar. Men who have betrayed or embarrassed him previously could not depend on his desire "to be fair."

He then announced he could no longer withhold the sword. "Today, in one of the most difficult decisions of my Presidency, I accepted the resignations of two of my closest associates in the White House—Bob Haldeman, John Ehrlichman—two of the finest public servants it has been my privilege to know.

"I want to stress that in accepting these resignations I mean to leave no implication whatever of personal wrongdoing on their part, and I leave no implication tonight of implication on the part of others who have been charged in this matter."

Well then, what was it that he was doing? Why was he stripping himself of his two closest associates? They did not want to resign. They had been urging him to "tough it out." Surely the only reason for such drastic action was that they had committed *some* wrongdoing. In fact, he had already said they had been concealing the truth from him on criminal matters.

Then holding the banner of official integrity at its proper level, he explained why impeachment was a reasonable remedy for all those involved.

"But in matters as sensitive as guarding the integrity of our democratic process, it is essential not only that rigorous legal and ethical standards be observed, but also that the public, you, have total confidence that they are both being observed and enforced by those in authority, and particularly by the President of the United States."

Then in a half-confession of previous error, he went on to say it would never happen again. "Whatever may appear to have been the case before, whatever improper activities may yet be discovered in connection with this whole sordid affair, I want the American people, I want you, to know . . . that during my term as President justice will be pursued fairly, fully and impartially, . . ."

So low had his reputation fallen that polls taken immediately after the speech indicated a majority of the American people did not believe him.

Then ignoring that he had already blamed his subordinates for deceiving him, and, indeed had confirmed their guilt by requesting their resignations, he struck the pose of a noble boss, ready to accept all responsibility.

"For the fact that alleged improper actions took place within the White House or within my campaign organization, the easiest course would be for me to blame those to whom I delegated the responsibility to run the campaign. But that would be a cowardly thing to do."

Although he had already done it, he did not want people to think he was capable of such "cowardly" behavior.

"I will not place the blame on subordinates, on people whose zeal exceeded their judgment and who may have done wrong in a cause they deeply believed to be right. In any organization the man at the top must bear the responsibility.

"That responsibility, therefore, belongs here in this office. I accept it."

But he had previously asked, "Who, then, is to blame?" He was not accepting the blame for setting in motion the domino action which was threatening his impeachment, he was merely accepting the responsibility for the action of others.

And then, to underscore that he was taking on none of the blame, he said, "And I pledge to you tonight from this office that I will do everything in my power to insure that the guilty are brought to justice."

Now that he had cleared this up he must turn to other matters. "Since March, when I *first learned* [italics added] that the Watergate affair might in fact be far more serious than I had been led to believe, it has claimed far too much of my time and my attention. Whatever may now transpire in the case . . . I must now turn my full intention [sic]—and I shall do so—once again to the larger duties of this office."

There were so many things for him to do. The German chancellor was going to visit with him the next day. There was a meeting with the Russians for which he was going to have to prepare. The Middle East and Southeast Asia also needed his attention. Last, but not least, he had to start worrying about America. Inflation was getting out of hand. It was a shocking 8% per annum. Housewives were upset.

Then he went on to tell of the goals for his second term he had written down at Christmas time. "But we cannot achieve these goals unless we dedicate ourselves to another goal. We must maintain the integrity of the White House.

"And that integrity must be real, not transparent.

"There can be no whitewash at the White House."

He then started the whitewash by smearing his political opponents. After observing one of the central lessons about Watergate, "Two wrongs do not make a right," he proceeded to justify himself by showing how wrong his opponents had been.

"I know that it can be very easy under the intensive pressure of a campaign for even well-intentioned people to fall into shady tactics, to rationalize this on the grounds that what is at stake is of such importance to the nation that the end justifies the means.

"And both of our great parties have been guilty of such tactics.

"In recent years, however, the campaign excesses that have occurred on all sides have provided a sobering demonstration of how far this false doctrine can take us."

There was a false doctrine here, but it was a false doctrine of his making. No one had accused the Democrats of the crimes now being openly confessed by the Republicans. It was as a result of Richard Nixon's orders that spies had followed family members of Democratic candidates and assembled dossiers on their private lives. The Democrats had not forged letters and had them distributed under the letterheads of the Committee for the Re-election of the President. They had not leaked false information to the press, and manufactured misleading ads. They had not bugged Republican National Committee headquarters, seized confidential files, sabotaged campaign schedules and agitated groups, by means of provocateurs, to behave in a manner to discredit their opponents. In short, they had not done what Richard Nixon had attempted to do, namely, steal a national election.

"The lesson is clear," he said, "America in its political campaigns must not again fall into the trap of letting the end, however great that end is, justify the means."

Substitute the name Richard Nixon for *America* in

that egomaniacal paragraph and one lesson about Watergate does become clear.

It was an unconvincing, sanctimonious, frequently illogical speech. He delivered it nervously, as is his style. Towards the end he indicated that being President was not all that much fun any longer. Like any convict crossing off days on the calendar until he would be released, he confided that he had ascertained that morning there were only 1,361 days left before he would be out of office. And then, as if to signal how little pleasure he expected during that time, he piously said, "Tonight, I ask for your prayers to help me in everything that I do throughout the days of my Presidency."

Finally, after a long pause, he said, "God bless America. And God bless each and every one of you."

After the speech, technicians in the room reported, he had brushed tears from his eyes and said, "It wasn't easy." He had a similar reaction at the end of the Checkers speech, when he threw his notes to the floor and told Pat, "I loused it up . . . I couldn't do it. I wasn't any good," then waved Chotiner off with "I was an utter flop," and rushed to the dressing room where he burst into tears.

This Checkers Speech II revealed that the President was determined to hang on, tell as little as he had to, maintain a façade of hurt innocence, and hope that there was enough gullibility around to let him slip by.

As the days passed it became evident his luck and credibility had run out. By mid-May his standing in the polls had fallen to an all-time low. Only 45 per cent of those polled thought he was doing a good job. That faithful number was declining each day.

Perhaps the chief instrument in his humiliation was Sam Ervin's Senate Select Committee. On May 17 the committee began to hold public sessions. The extraordinary power of television to add meaning to democratic participation was immediately demonstrated. Millions of people watched and judged as the minions told their fragmented, yet condemning stories.

They spoke of doing it all because they thought the

Attorney General wanted them to do it, and if he was so disposed, then surely the President wanted it done. Even these minor figures knew enough about Watergate to make the case against the President circumstantially sound.

What would happen when Jeb Magruder appeared and when John Dean told all he knew?

These were frightening prospects. Yet he knew that the best strategy in this situation, the strategy he had been pursuing for eleven months, was to remain as silent as possible and hope fickle public interest would be distracted by some other matter. He had said it in *Six Crises* when the slush fund scandal was threatening to destroy him: "The consensus that night among our little strategy group was to ignore the attacks, on the theory that answering them would simply give them more publicity and play into the hands of those making the attacks. This, I knew, was generally sound political strategy."

Sound political strategy for a Senator hoping to be bailed out by the incomparably popular Eisenhower was not necessarily sound political strategy for a President about whom everyone had his suspicions.

On May 19, ten days after he had been indicted by the grand jury, John Mitchell told United Press, "Somebody has tried to make me the fall guy, but it isn't going to work."

There was a mortal threat implicit in those words and they helped drive Richard Nixon into his next act of desperation.

# CHAPTER XV

## Nixon's Confession

Alone now, the ranks of his faithful staff thinned to the point where Ron Ziegler represented the most familiar face, Nixon felt as he always had, a man in battle who could depend only on himself.

The battle image was all important to him. On April 20, when trying to reassure the Cabinet, he had said, "We have had our Cambodias before." To his mind it was simply a matter of holding on until the tide of public opinion turned. Time and the indifference of distracted people were on his side. It did not matter that his associates had been caught in criminal acts inspired by him. People were going to be willing to believe the best of their President. Even if he was forced to confess all, he would know how to phrase it so that Americans would feel either sympathetic or impotent.

On May 22 he counterattacked. Reasonably sure he could not appear before the press without being torn by bitter remarks, perhaps even, as in Ron Ziegler's case, shouted at and called a liar, he issued a four-thousand-word "further statement."

In his April 30 speech to the nation he had deliberately avoided answering the questions which interested most people. He had named no names and limited his discussion to facts already made public. There was no new information. He had based his defense on the improbable idea that a seasoned politician such as himself had refused to believe anything he had read in the papers for months and had never doubted a single preposterous tale told to him by his staff. True, he had abandoned the position that no one in his administration was involved, in favor of the proposition that both parties had always been equally involved in such behavior.

181

But he had not explained why it had happened or how so many men in his administration turned out to have such weak characters that "zeal" would make them dishonor themselves.

On May 22 he changed tactics. He revealed a great deal which had never previously been suspected, and in the process wrote the first Presidential confession. Such charges of corruption, police state techniques used to subvert democratic institutions, criminal activity sanctioned by the head of state, and betrayal of trust had never been laid at the door of any President. It was Richard Nixon himself, expressing fears akin to paranoia, who presented the evidence on which all of the charges were based.

He immediately denied that what he was about to say about national security was intended as a subterfuge to shield his administration. "In citing these national security matters it is not my intention to place a national security 'cover' on Watergate . . ."

He then proceeded to use national security as a cover for Watergate. "Long before the Watergate break-in, three important national security operations took place which have subsequently become entangled in the Watergate case."

In short, Watergate would never have happened if "important" national security operations hadn't first forced him to act. The use of the modifier "important" was subjective. In *his* judgment it was important. Others did not agree—among them, he was soon to admit, J. Edgar Hoover. Yet his use of authoritarian excesses and criminal behavior were about to be justified on the basis of this, and similar loaded words.

"The first operation, begun in 1969, was a program of wiretaps." Simple. From the moment he came into office he had been engaged in an operation which many considered illegal, and which the Supreme Court unanimously outlawed two days after the Watergate break-in. Why was this done?

"They were undertaken to find and stop serious national security leaks." There was the cover again. And

there again was the modifier, "serious." Other men
characterized the leaks as unimportant. They involved
administration thinking about disarmament. Surely the
Russians were not surprised at any information they
found in the *New York Times*. Lending substance to this
conclusion is the fact that a treaty satisfactory to us *was*
signed.

He wanted Americans to know that, although they
may have been illegal, his domestic wiretaps "produced
important leads that made it possible to tighten the security of highly sensitive materials."

But Dr. Kissinger, whose staff members were bugged
with his permission and who read the transcripts of their
conversations, said the taps had proved all his associates
were loyal. The President confirmed that Kissinger had
indeed read the transcripts. "Information thus obtained
was made available to senior officials responsible for national security matters in order to curtail further leaks."
Since these men were not the source of the leaks, how
had the tapping of their phones curtailed further leaks?
As in the case of much of what he said, the details were
lacking. It was a matter of accepting his assurances that
he was justified. In view of the numerous examples of
"inoperative" statements he had been issuing for months,
it was difficult to take such assurances at face value.

"The second operation was a reassessment, which I
ordered in 1970, of the adequacy of internal security
measures. This resulted in a plan and a directive to
strengthen our intelligence operations."

This was, by any standard but his own, an illegal plan.
"The options initially approved had included . . . authorization for surreptitious entry—breaking and entering, in effect—on specified categories of targets in specified situations related to national security."

These were exactly the activities practiced, solely for
political purposes, when Watergate became the "specified target."

It was astounding that a statement of this kind of
criminal intent had been written by the President of the
United States. What had driven him to this? Surely if he

suspected a crime was being committed, or even contemplated, he could have sent the Justice Department into court for a legitimate search warrant.

The imperatives which had driven him to this extreme during the spring and summer of 1970, he said, were "bombings" on college campuses and in some cities. Specifically he had been upset because "there were four hundred bomb threats in one twenty-four-hour period in New York City." Since by themselves the city's nine hundred schools, none of which have ever been bombed, can expect an average of one bomb threat a day during the spring solstice, this was hardly as serious a matter as he made it out to be.

Furthermore, he had been upset by "violence on college campuses," and also "the tragedies at Kent State and Jackson State." That year, he pointed out, "brought nearly eighteen hundred campus demonstrations, and nearly two hundred fifty cases of arson on campus. Many colleges closed." The college kids had obviously gotten under his skin, but was that sufficient reason to decide that "surreptitious entry—breaking and entering" —were justified?

Finally, he said ominously, "Gun battles between guerrilla-style groups and police were taking place." He was making it sound like the Sierra Maestre just before Castro seized power. But what he seemed to be referring to again was the isolated tragedies of Kent and Jackson State Colleges.

Then, in order to demonstrate how serious the situation really was, he said, "Some of the disruptive activities were receiving foreign support."

This was an extremely serious charge. This required substantiation. None was forthcoming.

What possible reason did he have for failing to identify the source of this "foreign support." Surely if such support existed, the country that had supplied it was our enemy and there was no reason to hide its identity. In addition, simply mentioning this *support* was enough to alert the enemy that our intelligence agents had uncovered their apparatus. In short, the only ones being kept in the dark were the American people, who were being asked to excuse the inexcusable on the grounds of some phantom national security consideration.

But, the President wanted everyone to know, they had nothing to worry about. America, contrary to what he had just revealed, was not moving in the direction of a police state. All because J. Edgar Hoover, the hobgoblin of the Left, had not let it happen. On June 5, 1970, the President had created an inter-agency committee composed of the heads of the FBI, the CIA, Defense Intelligence, and the National Security Agency. The committee, under orders from the President, was to submit "a report which included specific options for expanded intelligence operations." These operations were all to be in the *domestic* sphere. By participating the CIA was instantly in violation of its Congressional charter.

The report, suggesting surreptitious entry, was submitted to the President on June 25, 1970. The President took a month to carefully consider its implications. He then gave it his approval—or, as he put it, "the agencies were notified by memorandum of the options approved."

However, Hoover disapproved. He informed the President that unless he ordered him to take part in this clandestine operation *in writing,* he would have no part of it. The President, recognizing the potential for blackmail in this bureaucratic request, retreated. Or, as he put it, "After reconsideration, however, prompted by the opposition of Director Hoover, the agencies were notified five days later, on July 28, that the approval had been rescinded."

Although this resolve to employ burglary techniques was not implemented in 1970, it exposes the mentality that went into planning and executing the break-ins at Watergate and Dr. Fielding's office, and the proposed burglary of Senator McGovern's offices.

Since this reflected poorly on President Nixon, why was he revealing it? The explanation for this incomprehensible act of self-immolation was not long in coming.

"It was this unused plan and related documents that John Dean removed from the White House and placed in a safe deposit box, giving the keys to Judge Sirica."

He had concluded, apparently, that if he did not first speak of this matter in terms of pressing national security, John Dean would shortly speak of it in terms of a fresh scandal. It was a Hobson's choice of sorts. It was speak or be spoken of.

Apparently miffed at being used for purposes of which he did not approve, Hoover further tested the President's patience. "In July, 1970, having earlier discontinued the FBI's liaison with the CIA, Director Hoover ended the FBI's normal liaison with all other agencies except the White House." Hoover must have felt extremely provoked to go to this extreme. "To help remedy this," the President continued, "an Intelligence Evaluation Committee was created in December, 1970. Its members included representatives of the White House, CIA, FBI, NSA, the Departments of Justice, Treasury, and Defense, and the Secret Service.

"The Intelligence Evaluation Committee and its staff were instructed to improve coordination among the intelligence community and to prepare evaluations and estimates of *domestic intelligence* [italics added]."

Then, most cryptically: "I understand that its activities are now under investigation." No details, no elaboration, simply a caveat, as though to form a basis for some future claim that he had already spoken of this matter when the scandal finally came to light.

But in advance of that possibility, he wanted it known, "I did not authorize nor do I have any knowledge of any illegal activity by this committee. If it went beyond its charter and did engage in any illegal activities, it was totally without my knowledge or authority."

He was making a terrible admission of incompetence, with no indication he understood the meaning of his remarks. After first acknowledging their activities were "under investigation," he then boasted he did not have "any knowledge of any illegal activity by this committee." Was it he, the Chief Executive of the land, who had

authorized the establishment of this committee? Yes, of
course. Had he heard the committee might be engaged
in illegal activities? Certainly. Then why hadn't he gotten to the bottom of the matter? Why hadn't he ordered
the heads of these agencies into his office and demanded
an explanation instantly? Why wasn't he in a position to
reassure the public that their most sensitive police agencies had not been engaging in illegal activities? Or if
they had been engaging in such activities, why hadn't he
issued orders for them to stop? Why wasn't he able to
say that such transgressions would never again be allowed without the authorization of established legal
practices?

To this point he had confessed to an assortment of
bewildering entanglements, all of which had led to the
commission of crimes. However, there was more to
come.

"The third operation," the President continued, "was
the establishment, in 1971, of a special investigations
unit in the White House. Its primary mission was to plug
leaks of vital security information."

Again that judgmental word, "vital." He was now referring to the publication by the *New York Times,* and
subsequently most other papers in the country, of the
Pentagon Papers. Since the Supreme Court refused to
hold up the publication of these documents, and de-
escalation of the war continued at the pace President
Nixon had previously scheduled, it seemed like an inappropriate use of the word. Certainly, few people at
that time were shocked at what was revealed about Vietnam. It seemed like a difficult proposition to defend at
this late date, that the American people would have been
harmed if they knew everything there was to know about
Vietnam from the start.

What was shocking was what the President was about
to reveal. "I also directed this group [the Plumbers] to
prepare an accurate history of certain crucial national
security matters which occurred under prior Administrations, on which the Government's records were in-
complete."

In other words, he was going to have E. Howard Hunt draw up his own version of the Pentagon Papers, which, perhaps, he would then leak to the *Wall Street Journal*.

He had also implied that it had been his desire to fasten the blame for Diem's murder on John F. Kennedy. Hunt's cable forgeries took shape from this desire.

The publication of the Pentagon Papers, he claimed, caused all of his distress. "Other governments no longer knew whether they could deal with the United States in confidence." Again he was claiming too much. Leaks of information typified all government operations in most countries. In democracies, they very often act as an informal vehicle of information which self-protective politicians would prefer to keep from the public. The President had often taken part in this activity during his long political career. To suggest that China and Russia cared whether the American people were informed about what they were telling Henry Kissinger and Richard Nixon was to test the credulity of his listeners. Once having confided in Kissinger and Nixon, the secret was out. The only persons from whom the Chinese and Russians would have wanted to keep secret their thoughts were the leaders with whom they were going to have to negotiate. Their concept of democracy was not especially positive: once Nixon knew what was on their minds, it did not matter if "the suppressed masses" also found out.

But this is a matter of viewpoint, and the President claimed that this "security leak of unprecedented proportions" led him to an even more unprecedented act. Apparently having lost faith in the FBI and the CIA, "I approved the creation of a special investigation unit within the White House—which later came to be known as the 'Plumbers.' This was a small group at the White House whose principal purpose was to stop security leaks and to investigate other sensitive security matters. I looked to John Ehrlichman for the supervision of this group."

This was a complete confession of complicity in the Watergate break-in. For the President had previously recognized the principle that he could not shift the responsibility for his subordinates' acts. Furthermore, his subordinates had not created "the Plumbers." He had. In addition, he knew who they were and what they were supposed to do.

"Egil Krogh, Mr. Ehrlichman's assistant, was put in charge. David Young was added to this unit, as were E. Howard Hunt and G. Gordon Liddy. . . . I told Mr. Krogh that, as a matter of first priority, the unit should find out all it could about Mr. Ellsberg's associates and his motives. Because of the extreme gravity of the situation, and not then knowing what additional national secrets Mr. Ellsberg might disclose, I did impress upon Mr. Krogh the vital importance to the national security of his assignment."

In legal parlance, this is known as "a wink and a nod." Precise orders were not given to his impressionable, youthful aide, but he was left with the understanding that a true patriot would find some way to satisfy the President's "priority."

What further instructions Mr. Ehrlichman might have given Krogh the President was in no position to know. He had what the jargon popular in the White House at that time referred to as "deniability." He was in a position to say, as he did, "I did not authorize and had no knowledge of any illegal means to be used to achieve this goal."

He also revealed he had personally given them "additional assignments." In fact, they were kept busy until "the work of the unit tapered off around the end of 1971." Or put another way, their work tapered off at the White House when it picked up at the Committee for the Re-election of the President. But their duties did not change. They were still involved in planning "surreptitious entry—breaking and entering . . ."

At this point the President made a further confession. He prefaced it with the unconvincing insistence that "These intelligence activities had no connection with the break-in of the Democratic headquarters, or the aftermath."

He now stated the position he took after being *ap-*

*palled* at the news that his "Plumbers" had been caught in the Watergate.

"I considered it my responsibility to see that the Watergate investigation did not impinge ad: crsely upon the national security area. . . . Within a few days. however, I was advised that there was a possibility of CIA involvement in some way."

Who had so advised him? He did not say. "It did seem to me possible that . . . the investigation could lead to the uncovering of covert CIA operations totally unrelated to the Watergate break-in."

Well, if that was his concern, he had one legitimate course of action. He had only to lift the phone and ask Richard Helms whether his suspicions were true. He did not do that. Instead Haldeman and Ehrlichman, one scarcely believes without his knowledge, tried to bring pressure on the CIA to falsely claim such imaginary covert operations would be endangered if justice were allowed to run its course in the Watergate burglary.

Once General Walters informed them that no such threat to the CIA existed, and L. Patrick Gray passed this information on to the President, the only White House reaction to the news seemed to be disappointment.

The confession continued: "In addition, by this time, the name of Mr. Hunt had surfaced in connection with Watergate, and I was alerted to the fact that he had previously been a member of the special investigations unit in the White House."

He was finally admitting he had known about the White House connection to Watergate from practically the moment it happened. Even if he did not personally connect Hunt to the White House when his name was first mentioned, someone had brought that information to his attention. No wonder he had been appalled.

His immediate reaction was not to speed to the defense of justice; rather, it was to authorize the cover-up which was soon to destroy so many lives. "I was concerned that the Watergate investigation might well lead to an inquiry into the activities of the special investigations unit itself. In this area, I felt it was important to avoid disclosure of the details of the national security matters with which the group was concerned." The President was referring to forging cables and dredging up the torments of a troubled mind.

"I knew," he admitted, "that once the existence of the group became known, it would lead inexorably to a discussion of these matters."

He now tied himself in completely to the cover-up, accepting, for the first time, complete responsibility not only for knowing about the subsequent obstructions of justice, but for inspiring them.

"Therefore, I instructed Mr. Haldeman and Mr. Ehrlichman to insure that the investigation of the break-in not expose either an unrelated covert operation of the CIA or the activities of the White House investigations unit—and to see that this was personally coordinated between General Walters, the deputy director of the CIA and Mr. Gray of the FBI."

The purpose of this paragraph seemed clear. He was providing Haldeman and Ehrlichman with a defendable position on which to win out against any forthcoming indictment. They were merely carrying out his orders. He was brazenly admitting that he directed them to cover up. All the actions Magruder and Dean were attributing to Haldeman and Ehrlichman had been authorized by him.

He was, in effect, gambling that he could get away with acts which would undoubtedly land his cohorts in jail. The most serious possible threat to him would come if either Haldeman, Ehrlichman, or Mitchell turned on him. It was essential to protect them.

He knew the only real alternatives Congress had in the face of his admissions was to leave him alone or to impeach him. Attorney General Kleindienst told a joint session of three Congressional Committees on April 10 that, if they did not like what the President was doing, "You've got all kinds of remedies." Congress could "cut off our funds, abolish most of what we can do, or impeach the President,"

Richard Nixon had always been a plunger. The odds looked fairly good that Congress would not have the cohesiveness required to bring him before the bar. Those odds would lessen if any of those three men came to see their duty in a different light.

Then, boldly, he admitted what everyone knew. "On July 6, 1972, I telephoned . . . L. Patrick Gray. . . . During the conversation Mr. Gray discussed with me the progress of the Watergate investigation, and I asked him whether he had talked with General Walters. Mr. Gray said that he had, and that General Walters had assured him that the CIA was not involved. In the discussion, Mr. Gray suggested that the matter of Watergate might lead higher."

At this point he had bankrupted himself in the eyes of honest citizens. He had branded himself a liar. Not an inadvertent liar, but a monumental liar who, while lying, had looked every American in the eye on April 30. He had said that night:

"I repeatedly asked those conducting the investigation whether there was any reason to believe that members of my administration were in any way involved. I received repeated assurances that there were not."

Three weeks later he was saying, *"Mr. Gray suggested that the matter of Watergate might lead higher."*

Those Congressmen who reasonably wanted to have some proof the President knew of the cover-up, before considering impeachment, now had the proof from his own mouth.

In effect, he had also admitted that from July 6 on he knew the CIA was not involved. Therefore, one of his two main reasons for covering-up had disappeared. The only remaining one was that he wanted to keep secret his connection to the "Plumbers," since knowledge of their very existence might open up the possibilities their "sensitive" work would be exposed.

His resolve remained steady through the next ten months. "For example," he explained, "on April 18th, 1973, when I learned that Mr. Hunt, a former member of the special investigations unit at the White House, was to be questioned by the U.S. Attorney, I directed Assistant Attorney General Petersen to pursue every issue involving Watergate but to confine his investigation to Watergate and related matters and to stay out of national security matters."

Since he had defined all of the activity of the Plumbers, aside from Watergate, as "national security matters," he was telling Petersen—at the meeting in which Petersen first attempted to get permission to send news of the burglary of Dr. Fielding's office to Judge Byrne—that under no circumstances was he to do so. In this one statement he had confirmed that he was guilty of obstruction of justice.

Of course he had an explanation. It hinged on his contention national security depended upon his finding out whether a Harvard professor had Oedipal urges and a dead President could be implicated in a murder.

But then, most felons have rational explanations for their transgressions. They frequently find it difficult to understand why society cannot accept their plausible rationales.

In conclusion, he said, "It is clear that unethical, as well as illegal, activities took place in the course of that campaign." There was not a single word in his statement echoing his earlier assertions that the Democrats also behaved poorly.

However, he wanted people to believe, "None of these took place with my *specific* [italics added] approval or knowledge." What an incredible confession that one word was all by itself.

He went on, "To the extent that I may in any way have contributed to the climate in which they took place, I did not intend to; to the extent that I failed to prevent them, I should have been more vigilant."

A repentant sinner can depend on the sympathy of the congregation. However, *this* repentant sinner had no further sympathy for the Watergate transgressors. "It now appears that there were persons who may have gone beyond my directives, and sought to expand on my efforts to protect the national security in order to cover up any involvement they or certain others might have had in Watergate."

Too bad for them. The wink-and-nod boys were going to have to settle these matters "in the courts."

But whatever their fate, "the Watergate scandal should not be allowed to get in the way of what the administration sought to achieve." It was those wonderful *ends* again, which those wicked *means* should not be allowed to obscure.

Then, gritting his teeth, he stated, "Additional information may be forthcoming of which I am unaware. It is also my understanding that the information which has been conveyed to me has also become available to those prosecuting these matters."

Senator Ervin was seething after seeing some of the *information,* much of which was in the documents John Dean had given to Judge Sirica. On May 31 he said the White House plans showed a "Gestapo mentality." He wanted the Dean Papers made public and said, "It would be a great shock to the American people." According to Ervin the President's plans were to set up "an interagency operation to spy on Americans, especially those who disagree with the Administration."

The nature of Richard Nixon's fundamentally unAmerican attitudes was showing. His insecurity was so deep-seated that, at a minimum, he had apparently drawn up plans for bugging and wire tapping any persons he considered a personal threat.

The President prophesied as he ended his written statement, "As more information is developed, I have no doubt that more questions will be raised." He swore he would cooperate with all future efforts to find the truth.

He had been brought up to speak the truth. His mother had insisted on it. She often told a story which illustrated this point.

"It was during the Teapot Dome scandal," Hannah Nixon said, explaining how her son decided on his life's work. "Day after day the papers headlined stories of corruption in the handling of the government's oil re-

serves. One day, Richard—" Whether her son was in
the crib or in the White House, she addressed him only
in that formal manner. "—was lying in front of the fireplace, with newspapers spread all over the floor. Suddenly he said: 'Mother, I would like to become a lawyer
—an honest lawyer, who can't be bought by crooks.' "

That the vision of a nine year old can be distorted,
perhaps even lost, is suggested by Barry Goldwater's
cry of anguish published in the morally impeccable
Christian Science Monitor, April 11, 1973: "The Watergate, the Watergate. It's beginning to be like the Teapot
Dome. I mean, there's a smell to it. Let's get rid of the
smell."

It was time for Richard Nixon to join those men he
had sent on ahead for judgment and face the consequences for the "high crimes and misdemeanors" he had
committed against his countrymen.

# CHAPTER XVI

## *Articles of Impeachment*

When testifying before Congress April 10, 1973, on the question of President Nixon's possible abuse of executive privilege, Richard Kleindienst remarked, "You don't need evidence to impeach a President." All that was necessary, he indicated, was the votes.

The Attorney General was addressing himself, in his usual blunt political style, to an important legal question about which there has been some confusion.

An impeachment trial is a ceremony of awesome power. It is as though a group of men were placed back in Rousseau's "state of nature," with no laws to bind them, and asked to judge some member of the group with whose actions they are displeased.

But far from being savages in the field, these are the lawmakers of America. They have been chosen by their countrymen because of their merit and wisdom. In effect, they are a unique blue ribbon jury, composed mainly of lawyers, noted largely for their reflectiveness.

In their deliberation they are guided by no criminal statutes. They must answer to no higher authority. They need provide no justification for their decision. Their only guidelines are tradition and good sense.

As a result, the custom of the House of Representatives to draw up "articles of impeachment" tends to mislead. These articles, similar to the counts in a grand jury indictment, traditionally form the basis for the trial of the impeached individual. However, they are not, as is the case of a grand jury indictment, counts which must be measured against specific laws that the accused person has possibly violated. They are merely indications of areas of profound misbehavior, some of which may be the specific "treason, bribery and high crimes and misdemeanors" mentioned in the Constitution. Even those terms must be freshly defined each time in the minds of the Congressional jurymen.

*Although President Nixon has confessed to specific felonies, the confession was unnecessary. It was only required that his judges decide he had tacitly encouraged the crimes listed in his articles of impeachment, that he was involved in a scheme to obstruct justice, that he was neglecting his duty, in short that he was a man honorable and prudent men would not want to lead their country.*

Clearly there were aspects of the crimes of which he had no personal knowledge. However, he has admitted, if obliquely, to setting each of them in motion. Under those circumstances it is not necessary for him to have been caught with burglar tools in hand to be criminally tainted by every aspect of these transgressions and to become subject to impeachment.

When Andrew Johnson was called before the Senate, there were eleven formal charges in his articles of impeachment. On other occasions the number has been lower, one or two often sufficing.

In the case of Richard Nixon, the charges and their subdivisions—each of which is, in effect, an addition charge—could fill a small book. The list below is merely an outline of possible charges, to which members of the House Judiciary Committee would have little difficulty adding.

*Article I.* Illegal Wiretapping

1. Domestic wiretapping against newspaper personnel in 1969.

2. Wiretapping Democratic National Headquarters in the Watergate.

*Article II.* Conspiracy to Wiretap Illegally

1. The planning to commit these wiretaps.

2. The planning to tap Senator McGovern's headquarters.

*Article III.* Involving the Central Intelligence Agency in Domestic Espionage

1. 1970 inter-agency plans for domestic security.

2. Having CIA supply burglary devices for forceable entry into Dr. Fielding's office, August, 1971.

3. Having CIA draw up a profile on an American—Daniel Ellsberg.

### Article IV. Conspiracy to Involve the CIA in Illegal Domestic Activity

1. Attempting to get additional help for "Plumbers," during the summer of 1971, in Ellsberg case.

2. Attempting to get CIA to block FBI investigation of laundered Mexican money paying Watergate burglars.

### Article V. Involving the Federal Bureau of Investigation in Illegal Activity

1. Authorizing illegal domestic wiretapping in writing.

2. Directing that documents be removed from FBI file by agent.

3. Having L. Patrick Gray burn forged cables.

4. Ordering L. Patrick Gray to pass on Watergate reports to John Dean, who was involved in covering-up Watergate.

5. Urging the FBI to withhold information about the source and final use of money in Bernard Barker's account.

### Article VI. Burglary

1. Authorization, in 1970, of surreptitious entry—breaking and entering.

2. Dr. Fielding's office, 1971—stealing of files.

3. Watergate—stealing of documents.

### Article VII. Conspiracy to Commit Burglary

1. Plan to break into Senator McGovern's campaign headquarters after Watergate.

### Article VIII. Forgery

1. Creation of forged Diem cables.

2. Forged letter to the editor of *Manchester Union-Leader* accusing Senator Muskie of calling French Canadians "Canucks."

3. Charges, on Muskie letterhead, accusing Senators Jackson and Humphrey of sexual deviation in 1972 Florida primary.

4. Forged telegrams sent to White House on Haiphong bombing.

*Article VIII.* Bribery

1. ITT $400.000 donation to Nixon campaign in return for favorable ruling on Hartford Fire Insurance merger.

2. $400,000-plus milk industry contributions in return for reversal of price policy.

3. Oil money to Nixon campaign and rise in price of fuel oil, 1973.

4. Robert Vesco's $250,000 donation to Nixon campaign in exchange for Mitchell's influence in Lebanese Bank deal and SEC suit.

5. Payments to Watergate Seven to remain silent and plead guilty.

6. Parceling out ambassadorships for campaign contributions.

*Article IX.* Conspiracy

1. Meetings of Mitchell, Dean, Magruder, and Liddy, starting in January, 1972, and continuing until June, 1972, at which Watergate break-ins were planned.

2. Conspiracy to suppress information about Watergate.

3. Conspiracy to withhold information from Ellsberg jury.

4. Conspiracy to steal the 1972 Presidential election.

*Article X.* Breaking and Entering

1. The act itself at Watergate.

2. The act itself at Dr. Fielding's office.

*Article XI.* Obstruction of Justice

1. Failing to report break-in to Dr. Fielding's office in 1971.

2. Failure to report knowledge of Watergate break-in for eleven months.

3. Breaking open Hunt's White House safe.

4. Destroying contents of Hunt's safe.

5. Interfering with FBI and CIA investigations.

6. Ordering Assistant Attorney General Petersen to withhold evidence from Judge Byrne.

7. Payment of Watergate Seven to withhold evidence.

*Article XII*. Perjury

1. John Mitchell's denial he took part in bugging planning.

2. Jeb Stuart Magruder's false statements to the grand jury.

3. John Wesley Dean III's grand jury testimony.

4. Stans' denials of donations he had accepted to Nixon fund after April, 1972, disclosure deadline (at least three other counts).

5. Direct Nixon lies, confessed in the document of May 22, 1973.

*Article XIII*. Criminal Campaign Financing

1. Secret donations prior to April 7, 1972, which violate the 1925 act.

2. Vesco's undeclared $200,000.

3. Andreas' undeclared $25,000.

4. Destruction of donation and expenditure records.

5. Using campaign funds to support Watergate Seven.

6. Using campaign funds to pay for Watergate break-in.

7. Corporation donations.

*Article XIV*. Violating Mail Fraud Laws

1. Variety of activities conducted by Donald Segretti.

2. Sending false responses to radio station poll.

*Article XV*. Criminal Tax Violation

1. Authorizing the creation of four hundred fifty paper campaign committees, so that rich donors could divide gifts into $3,000 portions and avoid Federal gift tax.

2. Money paid to Watergate Seven as salaries was not declared as income and income tax was not paid.

*Article XVI*. False Statements to the FBI

1. Issued by most of the top members of the Nixon Administration.

*Article XVII*. Interference with the Electoral Process

1. Sabotaging Muskie's campaign.

2. Sabotaging Humphrey's campaign.

3. Sabotaging McGovern's campaign.

*Article XVIII.* Misusing Government Funds

1. Repairs on San Clemente home charged to government.

2. Payment of Hunt and Liddy while they were performing illegal acts.

*Article XIX.* Suborning Perjury

1. Urging grand jury witnesses to perjure themselves —Magruder and Watergate Seven . . . Herbert Porter . . . Hugh Sloan.

2. Urging Watergate Seven to lie during their trial.

*Article XX.* Tampering with Witnesses

1. Urging limitation of information by witnesses.

*Article XXI.* Misconduct in Public Office
(Counts too numerous to list.)

*Article XXII.* Attempts to Get Anyone to Attempt to Commit Any of These Crimes

*Article XXIII.* Concealing Knowledge of the Commission of Any of Them

(Each attempt can be treated as a separate offense.)

If the President is convicted at his impeachment trial, he is subject to no penalties except the forfeiture of his office and the prohibition of ever seeking public office again.

All of the laws cited above are, however, criminal in nature. Should the impeachment carry, the former President would be open to prosecution under their provisions, many of which are overlapping, all of which carry severe penalties.

# CHAPTER XVII

## A Call to Action

Some Americans have come to think of Presidents as elected monarchs, who have a specific term in office, during which time they are above criticism.

This undemocratic concept of leadership has been encouraged by some of the men who have recently occupied that office. There is something so tempting about being an object of worship, a repository of infallibility, that few of them have remained completely immune to its corrupting influence.

State dinners have become elaborate imperial displays, the White House band has been dressed up in Prussian uniforms, and *Hail To The Chief* has taken on the pomp of a monarchal trumpet call to clear the way and bow down.

For people who have succumbed to this mood, thoughts of impeachment are almost incomprehensible. The President, for them, represents the Presidency, the entire institution of American government summed up in one man, without whom the nation would collapse.

Perhaps if he were to go mad, setting fire to the Lincoln Room or taking pot shots at people passing along Pennsylvania Avenue, they would agree to impeachment; but, short of such a calamity, there he sits, regardless of what he does, for the duration of his reign.

This thought has perhaps been most forthrightly expressed by the Tory philosopher William Buckley. "In deference to the office of the Presidency, he [Nixon] must not be removed. Censured, yes; humiliated, yes. But to remove a President is to remove the sovereign."

This point of view would have outraged the patriots who founded this nation. Even such a pseudo-monarchist as Alexander Hamilton rejected that concept. "The

President of the United States would be an officer elected by the people for four years; the King of Great Britain is a perpetual and hereditary prince. The one would be amenable to personal punishment and disgrace; the person of the other is sacred and inviolable."

There is nothing more sacred or inviolable about Richard Nixon than there is about any other citizen. Like them he is susceptible to error and, like them, he is open to correction.

The very fact that a man who would be President is forced to expose himself to the people before he can enter that office, and must do so again in four years if he wishes to remain, is a mark of the mistrust the Founding Fathers placed in human nature. Prove that you are worthy, was their motto.

They had a deep suspicion of tyrants and sought to construct a form of government that would be resistant to man's corruptible nature.

One of the safeguards they provided in their structure for a more perfect union was the impeachment clause. They began to discuss it in Philadelphia on July 20, 1787. George Mason of Virginia led off:

"No point is of more importance. Shall any man be above Justice? Above all shall that man be above it who can commit the most extensive injustice?"

The country had been founded because Americans insisted that the principle of justice was more important than the fiction of royal infallibility. Was it reasonable, those arguing for an impeachment clause demanded, to assume that justice should be apportioned to everyone except the President?

James Madison, "the father of the Constitution," thought not. He argued for such a clause, insisting that it was "indispensable . . . for defending the community against the incapacity, negligence or perfidy of the chief Magistrate."

A majority agreed and, after a month and a half of reflection, settled down to write the final language. When it came before the Convention on September 8, the grounds for impeachment were confined to "treason and bribery."

This impressed the majority as too limited in scope. George Mason spoke for them: "Attempts to subvert the Constitution may not be treason." Then, as if to indicate how wide open he wanted the door of impeachment, he suggested the amorphous word "maladministration." In a mood of compromise he offered "other high crimes and misdemeanors."

Motivating the delegates was the thought that they must have an orderly method of removing a malevolent chief of state. Benjamin Franklin warned that unless there was provision for impeachment of an "obnoxious" President the people might be forced to rebel. Impeachment was to be a tool for strengthening the state, a method for making it function in an orderly manner. Without it some tyrant, some incompetent, might bring the operation of government to a halt.

The language Mason suggested, "high crimes and misdemeanors," was not intended to carry the same meaning as the phrase conveys when applied to criminal acts committed by individuals. It was taken directly from English law and was meant to conjure up the concept of *an offense against the state.*

Certainly criminal activity by a Chief Executive would represent such an offense, but so would a multitude of other sins not as easily defined.

There was no thought of applying impeachment proceedings casually. Although Richard Kleindienst's challenge to the Congress—that it could impeach the President if it disliked what he did—was true, it overlooked the tradition of American government.

Congress and the chief executive not only check and balance each other in an adversary relationship, they also accept the validity of each other's role. The President could always send troops to foreign wars and depend on Congress's unwillingness to go to the extreme of impeachment in order to stop him. But, until recently, Presidents seldom did that. They accepted limits on the exercise of their powers, some of which were not finally prohibited by the Constitution.

Nixon has pressed into new territory. He has constantly challenged Congress. Claiming to have ended the war in Vietnam "honorably," he proceeded to drop bombs on Cambodia at a rate unimagined in World War II.

If Congress did not appropriate money for something he wanted, he shifted money it had authorized for other projects to buy his pleasure. If Congress directed him to do something which did not strike his fancy, he ignored the legislative mandate.

He did this with the advice of a small group of "aides" who exercised fantastic, if informal, powers never envisioned in the Constitution. In the process, the Cabinet, whose members had to win the approval of Congress before receiving any power, was bypassed, and the business of the state was conducted under a cloak of secrecy which would have made the Borgias proud.

It still seems hard to believe that an administration sending up these kinds of warning signs could have for so long gone undetected in the commission of crimes to which the President has already admitted. It seems incredible that this kind of corruption was safely practiced until the District of Columbia police answered a routine call.

This is a unique situation in American history going far beyond a willingness to ignore Congress. It represents a willingness to use money criminally in order to hold on to power. It represents the substitution of official lying for official candor; for force over persuasion. The destiny of one man was placed above the destiny of the country. Government by the people and for the people was in the process of being replaced with government by Richard Nixon for Richard Nixon.

Faced with a crisis in his administration, he chose to misinterpret what was happening. "Some people," he said, "are saying the Watergate demonstrates the bankruptcy of the American political system."

Nonsense. Most people, including many members of his own party, were interpreting Watergate, and its ruinous accompanying scandals, as *his* moral bankruptcy.

Although Andrew Johnson was guilty of none of the charges brought against him in the nation's only Presidential impeachment, Richard Nixon's confession has made it clear that he is guilty as charged. Whereas the allegations against Johnson were transparently political, the admissions of Richard Nixon are specifically criminal.

This felonious, amoral political behavior is not part of the American system. It represents the failure of Richard Nixon, not the failure of American democracy. This is not politics as it is usually practiced, or was meant to be practiced, in the White House. This is Richard Nixon's brand of politics, as he has practiced it throughout his career. He has finally fought his way into a position where his lack of self-restraint and deficiencies of character have proven fatal.

The men around him knew that Nixon placed his own welfare before the welfare of the nation. When John Mitchell was caught, all he could think of in way of an explanation was that what he had been doing was "to try to get the President re-elected."

Loyalty to democratic ideals used to be the motor force driving men working in the White House. Loyalty to Richard Nixon had replaced it. Charles Colsen showed how far that degenerative process had gone when he wrote a memo to the White House staff eight weeks after the Watergate break-in:

"Think to yourself at the beginning of each day, 'What am I going to do to help the President's re-election today?' and then at the end of each day think what you did in fact do to help the President's re-election. . . . Just so you understand me, let me point out that the statement in last week's UPI story that I was once reported to have said that 'I would walk over my grandmother if necessary' is absolutely accurate."

What failings in Richard Nixon made him depend on

the services of a man who could write that sort of mindlessly immoral obscenity?

The men who would serve Nixon had to join the cult of personality and worship at his shrine. He would have it no other way. Some time early in life he confused his welfare with the welfare of the nation. As President he was in a position to blur that distinction still further.

Men of independent judgment and substance were hardly likely to accept such a distorted view of reality. This may explain Nixon's predilection for placing young men in positions of immense authority. One of his greatest transgressions was his exploitation of their youth, making them vulnerable, destroying their idealism and leaving them crippled by cynicism.

Working in the White House—which should have elevated all of them, enriched their lives, and prepared them for years of dedicated public service—left them, instead, with a facsimile of Dwight Chapin's empty credo: "The important thing is to protect the President."

For men of honor, the important thing had always been to protect the people and the institutions which serve them. But for the men around Nixon, that was subordinate to perpetuating him in office.

This flawed view of duty allowed Governor Ronald Reagan to object when the Watergate burglars were described as "criminals." "They were not criminal at heart," he insisted. "Their only aim was to re-elect the President."

The only aim of those interested in saving the Republic should be to deflate this overblown concept of the President as King. He was put in office to serve, not to be served.

Having violated that trust, he should be removed from office. Any person working for a living understands that principle as it operates in his own life. Why should the man who controls the destiny of the nation be judged against any lower standard?

Some men claim that in order to protect the office of the Presidency we must pretend that Richard Nixon is honest  The most audacious statement of that thought was made by former Secretary of Defense Melvin Laird, when he averred that if the President was really involved in the Watergate scandals, he did not want to know about it.

That kind of logic will destroy what it pretends to save. The country is faced with a unique danger. Accepting corruption at the summit of our system will encourage its growth in all the valleys of the land.

We have never before had a President who admitted uthorizing burglary. We have never had a President who admitted he obstructed justice. We have never had a President who tried to steal a national election.

Having made these confessions, he remains in office at our peril.

Men of conscience in the Congress must be guided by their oath to uphold the law. At stake is not the destiny of one man, but the destiny of the Republic. If they do their duty, Richard Nixon's greatest service to his country will be recorded in the centuries to come, when men look back to this moment with pride.

A wound has been inflicted against our system of government. It will not heal until the dirt has been cleansed from it. In its treatment, there is no stronger medicine than truth, no better guide than courage.

Richard Nixon has confessed to being a criminal and has challenged his peers to do something about it. They owe him the courtesy of an appropriate response.